Modern Witchcraft

*Unlocking the Secrets of the Norse Runes,
Divination, Spirit Guides, Tarot Reading,
Moon Spells, and Magic Rituals*

© Copyright 2024 - All rights reserved.

The contents of this book may not be reproduced, duplicated, or transmitted without direct written permission from the author.

Under no circumstances will any legal responsibility or blame be held against the publisher for any reparation, damages, or monetary loss due to the information herein, either directly or indirectly.

Legal Notice:

This book is copyright protected. This is only for personal use. You cannot amend, distribute, sell, use, quote, or paraphrase any part or the content within this book without the consent of the author.

Disclaimer Notice:

Please note the information contained within this document is for educational and entertainment purposes only. Every attempt has been made to provide accurate, up-to-date, and reliable complete information. No warranties of any kind are expressed or implied. Readers acknowledge that the author is not engaging in the rendering of legal, financial, medical, or professional advice. The content of this book has been derived from various sources. Please consult a licensed professional before attempting any techniques outlined in this book.

By reading this document, the reader agrees that under no circumstances is the author responsible for any losses, direct or indirect, which are incurred as a result of the use of the information contained within this document, including, but not limited to, errors, omissions, or inaccuracies.

Your Free Gift
(only available for a limited time)

Thanks for getting this book! If you want to learn more about various spirituality topics, then join Mari Silva's community and get a free guided meditation MP3 for awakening your third eye. This guided meditation mp3 is designed to open and strengthen ones third eye so you can experience a higher state of consciousness. Simply visit the link below the image to get started.

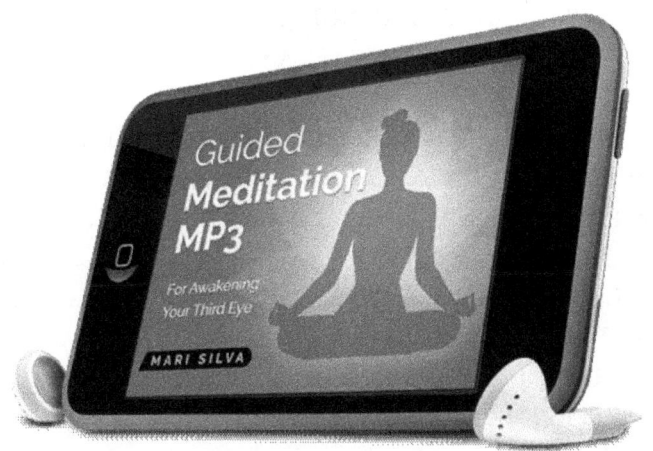

https://spiritualityspot.com/meditation

Table of Contents

INTRODUCTION 1
CHAPTER 1: WITCHCRAFT THROUGH THE AGES 2
CHAPTER 2: WITCHCRAFT FESTIVALS AND BELIEFS 12
CHAPTER 3: THE ELEMENTS 22
CHAPTER 4: GODS AND GODDESSES IN WITCHCRAFT 32
CHAPTER 5: TAROT CARDS 46
CHAPTER 6: RUNIC DIVINATION 54
CHAPTER 7: CRYSTAL DIVINATION 67
CHAPTER 8: LUNAR MAGIC 79
CHAPTER 9: SPIRIT GUIDES 89
CHAPTER 10: RITUAL MAGIC 99
BONUS CHAPTER: THE HERBAL GLOSSARY 106
CONCLUSION 110
HERE'S ANOTHER BOOK BY MARI SILVA THAT YOU MIGHT LIKE.. 111
YOUR FREE GIFT (ONLY AVAILABLE FOR A LIMITED TIME) 112
REFERENCES 113

Introduction

Don't we all deserve a bit of magic in our lives? Have people become so focused on science and technology that they have lost the ability to think beyond the regular world and wonder what is out there in other realms? Human ancestors knew the importance of having an open mind and acknowledging that higher energies and beings exist outside their regular sphere of knowledge. They developed tools, spells, and rituals that asked these higher beings to come into their lives and bring their powerful energy with them.

Of course, some of these practices focused on negative energies. They were classed as Satanism or working with the devil, but these examples shouldn't give witchcraft a bad reputation. Modern society is beginning to seek out more supernatural forces and make them part of regular life, and why shouldn't you? Consider the word supernatural. Nature is amazing, and we all recognize that fact, so imagine tapping into a SUPER natural source. How amazing would that be?

You are about to discover how to be more in touch with yourself, your subconscious, and the array of natural and supernatural energy sources available. You have the control and means to explore these sources safely and with the knowledge that you can improve your life. Great things are out there, and why shouldn't you have them? Be part of the world of magic and discover your spirit team, who has been waiting for you since before your conception. They are benevolent and loving and will soon become part of your life. Are you ready to jump in and get started? Let's go!

Chapter 1: Witchcraft through the Ages

Witchcraft Timeline

Early mankind needed to find ways to survive. They needed shelter and food to keep their communities safe and healthy. Imagine being a hunter-gatherer back then, and you had to find ways to bring home food for your group. No information was available about how to trap your prey; you had to use the materials at hand. Early mankind used magic rituals involving the fertility of humans. They would attract animals by wearing the skins of their kills topped with antlers or horns to show their strength and leadership.

Shamans held elaborate ceremonies to thank the goddess of the hunt.
Metropolitan Museum of Art, CC0, via Wikimedia Commons:
https://commons.wikimedia.org/wiki/File:%22Diana,_Goddess_of_the_Hunt%22,_Folio_from_t he_Davis_Album_MET_DP107569.jpg

    Magic men or shamans would hold elaborate ceremonies to thank the goddess of the hunt and the mistress of the herds and fish. One of the first depictions of early witchcraft was found in the French Pyrenees and named the Dancing Sorcerer. A magical being with human feet, the large round eyes of an owl, the genitalia of a large feline, and the tail of a horse or wild dog, all topped with the impressive antlers of a stag. The figure also had the front paws of a lion and was covered in animal skins. The image is believed to date back to 1400 BC and is believed to be the earliest record of witchcraft ever found.

As man became more developed and entered the Neolithic period, the Moon and the triple cycle of magic began to influence man's practices. Images of the triple goddess and the cycle of fertility became more important. Men had begun to rely more on agriculture to feed their communities, and the focus of their magic changed accordingly. A trio of stone statues dedicated to the Triple Goddess, the maiden, the mother, and the crone, were found in caves in France and are thought to have originated between 1100 BC and 1300 BC.

The more traditional timeline of witchcraft began back in Egypt and ancient Sumerians, where artifacts suggest that witchcraft and magic were important, and books of spells from around 3000 BC contained magic incantations and rituals dedicated to bringing back the dead and protecting the living.

The Bible also refers to multiple witches, divination, and the complex powers of magic. The Witch of Endor is called upon to consult with King Saul, and she predicts the death of Saul and his sons in a battle against the Philistines. The following day, Saul's sons were killed on the battlefield, and Saul was so distraught he took his own life. These references are believed to originate from around 900 BC. They are just a few of many references to the craft and magic that were common then.

Empress Wei, who ruled from 129 BC to 91 BC, was accused of practicing dark magic to help her get pregnant in China. She was exiled from the capital city along with hundreds of people helping her, and all of them were executed for their part in practicing witchcraft. The Romans and Greeks were also responsible for crediting witchcraft, and the Romans believed it was a certified practice that was a positive way to perform magic, while the Greeks viewed the craft more negatively.

In America, witchcraft was a heady mix of cultural beliefs, with Hoodoo, Voodoo, and Christianity all part of the melting pot. Slavery meant that African-based beliefs started to become part of the American culture and blended with more traditional beliefs to form the witchcraft that people believed in and performed. Many displaced cultural groups used witchcraft to make their lives more acceptable and fight back against their perceived place in society. The spells were often cast to improve their lives and fight against the endemic injustices the slaves faced and fought back against the masters and slave owners who controlled them. The Christian beliefs were upheld to mask the original craft and eventually became part of how magic is used today.

The Middle Ages was the most documented era of witchcraft, and many historians focused on the hunts and the trials that practitioners faced. In the 16th century and the years leading up to the era, magic was considered an acceptable practice and was part of regular worship and beliefs. Even the Church considered magic nothing more than superstition - nothing to be feared or even recognized - while the rest of the population believed and performed many forms of magic and witchcraft until the Church changed its perceptions.

In 1484, the Church changed its stance in an attempt to convince the populous that Pagan beliefs and magic were evil and that the only beings capable of such magic were God and the Holy Spirits. They issued an edict stating that witches were real and should be hunted down and held responsible for their evil practices. Throughout Europe, texts were written describing how to spot these evil witches and what to look for. Witch hunters were appointed to rid the communities of supposed witches and the people who supported them. Single older women were especially vulnerable to scrutiny, and women who lived alone were also under suspicion.

The rise of Protestantism also contributed to the furor, and both Catholics and Protestants formed committees and juries to try witches and send them to their fate. Religion played such a huge part in society that witches and their persecution were high on everyone's radar, leading to a system of fear and suspicion. A single rumor could start a major campaign against individuals or even families, and many people lived in fear of being persecuted. At the height of the witch panic, it is thought that between 40,000 and 50 000 people were executed, most female.

As the European panic subsided, the witch culture traveled across the ocean and found a new home in the Colonies. America was already a boiling pot of cultural influences when the town of Salem became the center of the new witchcraft superstitions. Three women were accused of being witches and started a maelstrom of accusations and persecution; these hearings are now called the Salem Witch Trials. The women were accused of casting spells that led to the possession of three girls in the town, which caused them to become the Devil's tools. The daughter of the Reverend Paris and her two cousins were acting irrationally and suffering from unexplainable fits, and the girls claimed that Sarah Good, a poor elder; Sarah Osbourne, a homeless beggar; and the Reverend's indentured servant Tituba were all guilty of witchcraft.

Tituba confessed to the crime and was pardoned, while Osbourne died before trial, and Good was hanged. She became the first "witch" to be executed on American soil, and her death led to a wave of paranoia and suspicion that spread through the Colonies rapidly. Over 200 people were accused, and at least 20 were executed. The situation was quelled in 1693 with a letter from Benjamin Franklin labeling the situation as ridiculous and having no basis in truth. In Europe, 1700 also marked an end to the superstitions and fear surrounding witchcraft. It led to laws being passed that stated that anyone who claimed to be a witch would be charged with fraud because witches weren't real and had no power.

While witchcraft never really disappeared, the hysteria surrounding it was dispelled, and other religions and beliefs became more prevalent. In the early 1920s, an English scholar who studied and taught Egyptology published a book called "The Witch Cult in Western Europe' in which she claimed that witches were practicing animal and child sacrifices and those covens led by the Devil himself were part of the culture and existed across Europe. However, she published a further book in the 1930s that changed her perceptions and proclaimed that witchcraft was the ancient religion that predated Christianity and should be included in modern culture.

It was in the 1950s that the resurgence of Paganism started to catch on with the emergence of Gerald Gardner and his book Modern Witchcraft. He started a movement known as Wicca and consulted with the infamous Aleister Crowley to create rituals, spells, and other magical pagan traditions that worked with the seasons, equinoxes, and solstices. In 1953 Gardner appointed an English woman, Doreen Valiente as his high priestess of the coven known as Bricketwood Coven. She was an influential figure who had been practicing magic since childhood and was an accomplished advocate of Wicca.

Doreen went on to become one of the most influential voices of modern magic, and she wrote five books about the craft. Her work encouraged readers to do more research and advocated that Wicca could be practiced by anyone and everyone without being initiated and part of the official Wicca movement. Her legacy was described as "The Mistress of Modern Magic," and she encouraged the growth of Wicca until her death in 1999.

Modern Witchcraft Today

Wicca and other pagan beliefs have become more popular since the 1970s, and more people are turning to alternative religions rather than conforming to traditional ones. They are embracing nature-based magic and using pagan traditions to mark the changes in seasons and how to live with the magic of nature. People are leaving more traditional religions and embracing spirituality instead. They prefer to distance themselves from established churches that have been connected to scandals and beliefs that limit what their followers can do. Religion is judgmental, and millennials aren't prepared to be told by anyone what they should do and what punishments they face if they choose another path.

Millennials are well-informed and unrestricted by their choices. They know what is out there and can connect to the rest of the world with just a click of a button. Information about Hinduism, Wicca, Buddhism, and other religions and belief systems is easily accessible, and they can chat with practitioners worldwide. This is both liberating and paralyzing, as too many choices could mean they fail to choose because they fear making the wrong choice. Spirituality, a blanket term, gives them the freedom to work with others dedicated to casting off consumerism and working together to make the world a better place.

Witchcraft has been expanded to include many different practices to suit modern society. New-age witches are everywhere, and they no longer have to fear society. They practice in full view or in their homes depending on their preferences and are part of the new belief system that is more inclusive and far thinking.

Types of Witches

First, let's eliminate the horror story image of witches with warty faces and scary green skin that are intent on capturing the innocent princess. Witches aren't occult or servants of the Devil, but they are supernatural. What is supernatural? Traditionally supernatural means a phenomenon that is beyond the laws of nature and scientific understanding, but in witchcraft terms, it can be more literal. Witches are supernatural because they work with and understand the natural world's power and how to use them. Modern witches look like everybody else and are often accomplished healers who work with nature to bring magic to the world.

They are not outcasts; they are accepted in society, and all identify with certain characteristics. Look at the list below and see if you can identify with witchcraft or if you recognize any that seem familiar.

Traditional Witches

Often referred to as folk witches, these practitioners will often work in covens and practice more traditional spells. They prefer to work with older spirits connected to their region and are knowledgeable about the craft through the ages. If you meet a traditional witch, you will learn a lot about the origins and history of witchcraft and the literature created.

Ceremonial Witches

These practitioners are more secretive than other witches who work with ceremonial magic. They believe in the power of high magic, and their practices have a certain pecking order. Ceremonial witches attain self-esteem from their magic and intend to become more accomplished and learned.

Kitchen Witches

One of the more popular forms of witchcraft involves performing magic in the heart of the house and the kitchen. Kitchen witches create potions and food to heal and bring luck and love to themselves and their loved ones. They will often be accomplished gardeners and have a sustainable source of ingredients in their homes. Kitchen witches work with seasonal ingredients and follow recipes passed down through their families for generations.

Green Witches

Also called forest witches, these practitioners work outside with the magic of nature. They have a deep knowledge of plants and herbs and a powerful connection with the elements. The green witch will often work with kitchen witches and collaborate to make healthy and magic dishes and potions from their ingredients.

Hearth Witches

Another form of the craft centers on the home. Everybody knows that the hearth is the traditional place in the home where the family gathers and shares their experiences. Hearth witches are often skilled crafters and use natural products and materials to create their magic. They use their skills to bring positive and healing energy to themselves and their homes. Even though most modern homes don't have traditional hearths, this kind of witchcraft is still effective and popular.

Hedge Witches

Although the name suggests some connection to greenery, the hedge means something different in magic. The hedge is the barrier between this world and the spiritual realm. Hedge witches have experienced communicators and will use their magic to speak to the spirits and bring their messages back to this world. They use astral traveling or lucid dreams to form their connections. They are adept at separating their soul from their physical body so it can travel between the two worlds.

Some cultures refer to this type of witch as a shaman, seidh, or an astral witch.

Cosmic Witches

These witches use astrology and astronomy to power their magic. They draw energy from the stars and the skies, using that energy to perform rituals and cast spells. Cosmic witches will study natal charts and use the alignment of the planets and stars to guide them during their work. Cosmic witchcraft involves a lot of details and appeals to people who believe in the power of the cosmos.

Augury Witches

These witches rely on their magic to see the future and divine what may occur in the future. They use omens, tarot cards, and other tools to seek signs, and they can also work with animals and the natural world. Augury witches often fall into trances and meditative states when they perform their magic and will work with the spirit world and nature to create their visions and messages,

Norse Witches

These witches follow the ancient Norse traditions and study Odin and Freya. The Norse religion of Asatru is filled with magical connections and powers that originated from the old Gods and Goddesses that form the beliefs they follow today. Asatru is popular because followers don't worship their deities. They believe they have human qualities and are as prone to making mistakes as regular men. Norse legends often depict them as drunken buffoons or brawling idiots who can be tricked and led astray. These human qualities make them some of the more approachable deities in pagan beliefs and help their popularity.

Elemental Witches

These witches work with elements and cast their spells using the power of nature. Later in the book, the elements and their place in witchcraft will be examined more closely.

Faery Witches

The Fae are mythical fairy-like creatures that appear in Celtic mythology and are representative of natural phenomena. The witches connect to the creatures and draw energy from them to fuel their magic. This type of practice is related to green witchery but concentrates on the faeries as well as the connection they have to nature.

Lunar Witches

Like cosmic witches, these practitioners focus on the skies, particularly the moon. They use rituals and spells filled with lunar energy, and the spells they cast will be explained later in the book.

Solar Witches

These witches use the sun's power to energize their tools and spells. They channel the sun to bring light and positivity to their magic. They will often perform their rituals or magic at sunrise or sunset so that these are enhanced by solar energy.

Sea Witches

These witches work with the power of water, especially the sea. They work with spirits and entities that live in the waves and have rituals that connect them to certain deities. Their environment often dictates the magic of sea witches, and they will also work using other bodies of water, such as lakes and rivers.

Secular Witches

These witches don't believe in divine blessings or powers. They have no connection to deities or religious bodies and believe solely in the power of ten natural worlds. This doesn't mean there aren't any secular religious witches. They may follow a religion but separate the two parts of their lives so magic and religion don't influence each other.

Chaos Witches

These witches embody the natural chaos of the world. They believe that creating loud and conflicting energies fuels their magic. Many witches practice in calm and serene conditions that help them connect to the spirits, but chaos witches do the opposite. They make loud noises and thrive on the energy that they create. They also work well with turbulent weather and love to perform rituals in storms and chaotic meteorological conditions. Beware the chaos witch, as they normally favor curses and hexes in their practice, so if you anger them, you may feel their wrath.

Eclectic Witches

These witches practice multiple kinds of magic and are always open to new ideas. Eclectic is an umbrella term to describe witches who embrace different forms of the craft. They understand that natural connections lead to commonalities in magic. For instance, the lunar witch and the sea witch will share certain energies because the lunar cycles affect the sea.

Whichever type of witch you identify with is fine. There are no hard and fast rules about your beliefs and where you draw your energy from. Maybe you practice a witchery style that isn't mentioned here. That's also okay; just like the regular world, labels are less important than intentions. Call yourself whatever you like, as witches are powerful and important no matter what.

Chapter 2: Witchcraft Festivals and Beliefs

What Is the Wheel of the Year?

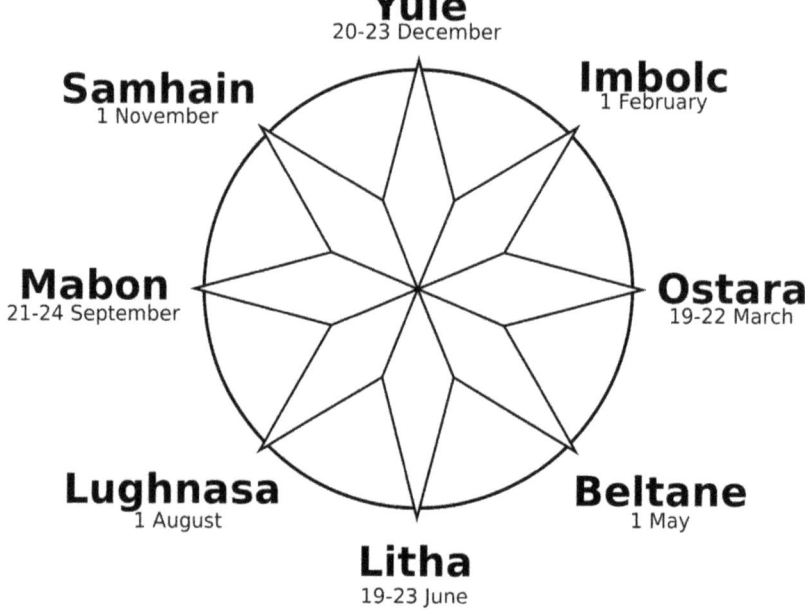

The Wheel of the Year shows nature's cycles, which form the basis of magic.
User: The Wednesday Island, after en:User:Brenton.eccles, Public domain, via Wikimedia Commons: https://commons.wikimedia.org/wiki/File:Wheel_of_the_Year.svg

When people hear about pagan rituals and witchcraft, they often think of dark rituals in the winter and summer solstice celebrations offering worship to perform dark magic and to connect with otherworldly spirits. In reality, the real wheel of the year is much more than a pagan calendar. Its origins date to pagan and neopagan cultures, but its real meaning is much more concerned with divine creation and the cycles of nature, which form the basis of magic and witchcraft. If you genuinely want to understand how your ancestors celebrated the seasons and the changing conditions in which they lived, you need to study the wheel of the year and the celebrations it represents.

Why do you look at the calendar? Birthdays, holidays, dentist appointments, and other mundane reasons are the main reasons people keep calendars but imagine how it was in pre-Christian times before the technologically advanced era. People who lived millennia ago didn't have the benefit of electricity and other modern power to rely on. When it went dark, there were only candles and fire to illuminate their homes, and when the weather changed, they needed to know what would and wouldn't grow to feed themselves. They needed bountiful harvests, and their knowledge of the cyclical changes in nature had to be part of that process to produce the food they needed when the seasons were favorable.

The wheel of the year is divided into eight sabbats representing points of the year that mark a shift in the season. They each have individual powers and characteristics that are celebrated accordingly. Some are solstices, equinoxes, and cross-quarter days, which are important milestones throughout the calendar year. Imagine the excitement and joy the community would feel as winter ended and fresh buds and spring flowers emerged. Imagine the hope and wonder when their animals began to produce offspring that would put meat on the family table and ensure their survival for another year.

Today the wheel of the year is less important. People eat imported foods, and the only way the seasons affect their lives is through what clothing they wear. Modern pagans, Wiccans, and other witchcraft groups are different. They understand that the power of nature is still cyclical and that the rituals and magic of the wheel of the year can help people to learn more about the natural world and how to care for it. No matter how hard you try to understand it, humankind is intrinsically linked to nature, and it isn't healthy to disconnect from it. It is spiritually fulfilling to cast off modern ways and retune your mind to nature and its changing seasons, so the wheel of the year is an effective guide to honoring nature's cycles.

The Eight Sabbats

Let's start with perhaps the best-known sabbat, Samhain. This is where the wheel of the year begins and the cross-quarter day that people recognize that summer has gone and the nights are starting to draw in.

Samhain 31st October – 1st November

Samhain evolved into All Hallows Eve or Halloween in more modern times, and, in some countries, children go out in fancy dress to "trick or treat" their neighbors and receive sweets and treats from them. The more traditional way to celebrate Samhain was to slaughter animals and store them in preparation for winter and to preserve other foodstuffs. The feast of Samhain represented taking stock and preparing for the cold months.

Samhain is when the veil between the living and the spiritual world is at its thinnest, and beings from the other world can cross easily to enter the physical world. Bonfires would be lit to cleanse the area, and the celebrants would leave food and drink to feed the spirits who visited. The Catholic Church adopted Samhain as All Hallows' Eve to mark a day to celebrate the dead and remember their time on Earth.

It is a time for reflection and taking stock spiritually. At Samhain, celebrate the return of darkness and heightened spiritual connections. Use the celebrations to mark endings and new beginnings so you can start afresh.

Correspondences

Nature: Squash and zucchini, pine cones, fungi, mushrooms, root vegetables.

Symbols: Squash and pumpkins for carving, skeletons, trees, ancestors, and the crone.

Colors: Red, black, brown, orange, and yellow.

Use the ingredients to make hearty stews and meals for yourself and your family. Batch cook meals in the freezer and preserve vegetables from your garden or the kitchen, so you don't waste anything. Make jam from leftover fruit and store it in your cupboards for winter.

Samhain Ritual

Decorate a room with relevant correspondences and pictures of your relatives who have passed. Light a single red candle and close your eyes. Ask the spirits of your ancestors to visit you and share their guidance on your life. Ask them to give you advice about specific areas and send you messages. The veil between the two worlds is at its thinnest and makes it the perfect time to connect with them.

Winter Solstice 21st December

Also known as Yule, this is the darkest point of the wheel. In modern terms, the 21st of December is the shortest day of the year and marks the end of the shortening of the days and longer nights. The ancients knew how special this time of year was and celebrated accordingly. They gave gifts, forgave moral transgressions, and offered sacrifices and gifts to the God Saturn. This is a time for transformation and rebirth, so magic centers around these energies. While the rest of the world prepares for Christmas, you can celebrate Yule by burning a Yule log and inviting your friends and families to your home for lavish feasts.

The winter solstice is a time for rest, and pagans look to nature for inspiration. The bees have sealed their hives and trees are bare and perennial plants are taking their nourishment from stored nutrients. Nature is taking a break, and you should do the same. Take the time to nourish your soul and mind by snuggling under blankets and reading. Eat heart food and replenish your energy.

Correspondences

Nature: Citrus, cinnamon, peppermint, rosemary, and sage

Symbols: Pine tree, holly, stars, logs, the hearth, reindeer, and candles

Colors: Red, gold, green, white, and silver

Yule Ritual

Light a red and green candle and ask the spirits to help you find peace. Close your eyes and reflect on the last year and what you achieved. Imagine a white light surrounding you and keeping you free from harm. Now take two deep breaths and feel peace descend and fill your body. Extinguish the candles and thank the spirits for their presence.

Imbolc 31st Jan – 1st Feb

This is the sabbat that celebrates the start of spring for pagans. As snowdrops break through the hard soil and the first signs of new life appear, it is time to celebrate rebirth. The sun has started to appear for longer, and it is time for you to welcome new projects and plant the seeds of intent. In agriculture, it is time to prepare the ground for the new planting cycle, and the same principles apply to witchcraft. Take the time to cleanse your magic tools and recharge them in the sun or moonlight.

Imbolc is the time to welcome back the light and celebrate the goddess, Brigid. She is the symbol of new life and is represented by a small cross made from woven rushes and placed at the door to the home. Connect to her by creating an altar related to Imbolc and asking her to send energy and love to you. She is the goddess of creativity and healing, so honor her by writing a poem or planting seeds to represent the rebirth of nature.

This is a magical time of the year and the perfect time to connect to nature. Grow your own herb garden or plant some hardy vegetables to celebrate your connection. Plant snowdrops and daffodils in your garden, or visit areas of natural beauty to welcome back the light into your life.

Correspondences

Nature: Snowdrops, daffodils, crocus, new potatoes, spring vegetables, fish

Symbols: The cross, straw dolls, flowers

Colors: White, yellow, pale blue, orange, silver

Imbolc Ritual

Create a sacred space on your altar or table and set three candles upon it. One white, one orange, and one green work well, but you can use whichever candles you have on hand.

Light them and close your eyes as you ask the spirits for the gift of light.

> *"Light the fire within my heart and let the light guide me,*
> *Step with me along the way and keep my spirit safe.*
> *Shadows that have ruled the land will now be gone.*

*And from their darkness, spring has sprung
And with its life and energy,
Let my life be renewed and bring me strength and force."*

When the candles have burned away, thank the spirits and finish the ritual.

Ostara or the Spring Equinox 21st March

Now nature is balanced, and there is an equal amount of light and darkness every day. Blossoms start to appear on the trees, and the chilly air of winter is but a memory. This is a time for hope, optimism, rebirth, and celebration. Ostara has inspired a lot of Easter traditions and customs, like egg hunts and the Easter bunny. Celebrate by creating colorful food and drinks that are filled with goodness. Share your home with friends and family and encourage crafting and nature hunts. Hide eggs in the garden so children and adults can have fun finding them and eating the spoils of their labor.

Correspondences

Nature: Daffodils, tulips, crocus, ducks, eggs, rabbits

Symbols: Eggs, hares, rabbits

Colors: Pastel yellow, pale blue, sea green, pink, purple

Ostara Ritual

Decorate your altar with eggs and rabbit toys, and place two yellow candles on the surface. Light them and ask the spirits to show you the power of rebirth. Ask them to fill your life with light and happiness and bring energy to you and your magic. Blow out the candles and thank the spirits for their assistance.

Beltane 1st May

This is truly the start of summer; the light expands, and long days beckon. Nature displays her nurturing side, and the world is green and abundant. The ancient pagans would have been filled with hope for the future, and two fires would be lit to bring cleansing smoke to their celebrations. Farmers would walk the cattle between the two fires before being led to summer pastures to graze. Cows would then jump over straw set on fire to prevent the fairies from stealing their milk.

Fires are a major part of Beltane celebrations, and young couples would leap over the flames to ensure conception. As the fires burned away, pregnant women would jump across them to protect their unborn children and bring them luck. The cooled embers would then spread across the sprouting crops to protect and encourage them to grow.

In modern times the celebration changed to May Day, but many old traditions still apply. The maypole can often be seen in village squares or smaller communities where the population gathers and dance. Maidens would dance and encourage young men to join them, while others would sell garlands of flowers to boost their dowry. May and Beltane are about nature coming to full bloom and is often associated with sexuality and conception.

Cast magic based on growth and fruition and celebrate the new life that is springing forward. Create a May doll dressed in white and decorated with flowers to adorn your house. Decorate your home with fresh flowers and bright ribbons to create a fun atmosphere, and invite your friends to BBQs and drinks so you can all look forward to summer together. Organize nature walks with friends and take notebooks and a pen to record and draw what you see.

Correspondences
Nature: Hawthorne, bluebells, berries, white roses, wisteria

Symbols: Garlands, flowers, the Maypole, the maiden, white flowers

Colors: Pale green, pastel yellow, pink, white, silver

Beltane Ritual
Decorate your altar with fresh flowers and white candles. Light the candles and ask for the spirits to bring love and romance to your life or to strengthen any current relationship. Ask for warmer and brighter weather to connect with nature.

Litha or the Summer Solstice 20th-21st June

The peak of the wheel. The days are at their longest, and the sun is strong. This is the sabbat to honor solar energy and perform magic connected with its power. The sun is the primary reason humans have life, so remember to honor the life-giving properties, and it is a time for outdoor celebrations with groups of people sharing their food. It is also a time for love and procreation, so celebrate your relationships and take advantage of the great outdoors.

Use natural ingredients to create tasty Litha treats like honey cakes or lavender cookies. Build a bonfire and celebrate the night sky in the warmth of its light. Litha is the time for exploration, so visit places that inspire you and bring you happiness. Go to the beach, feel the sun on your face as you dip your toes into the sea, and thank nature for its warmth. Go foraging for food and learn about the different bounties out there. Remember to check if plants are edible before you use them in your kitchen. Pick fruit from the elder tree and dry the fragrant white flowers to make cordial for fresh drinks or fry them in batter to make tasty fritters.

Correspondences

Nature: Elderflower, roses, lavender, tomatoes, spring onions, lettuce

Symbols: The sun, shells, fire, flowers, garlands,

Colors: Bright pink, yellow, gold, orange, turquoise, aquamarine

Litha Ritual

Take time to connect with nature by creating an altar in the garden. Add a bowl of fresh water, a yellow candle, and fresh flowers. Light the candle and close your eyes. Breathe in the fresh air and ask nature to bathe you in her light and positivity. Ask the spirits to bring prosperity and abundance to your life and inspire you to be more creative. Extinguish the candle and leave the altar with thanks and hope.

Lammas 1st August

The fruit is ripe, the crops are grown, and it is time to reap the rewards. Harvest is upon us, and it's time to enjoy nature's abundance. In magic terms, this means it's time to spend time with your loved ones and be powered by their energy. Your psychic abilities will be enhanced, and you will be more connected to high vibrations. Your connections will be at their best, and this is the time to connect with your spirit guides and ask them to guide you. Traditional English harvest festivals represent the way ancient pagans celebrated Lammas, where they brought gifts for the less fortunate members of the community.

Choose Lammas to volunteer your time at local homeless shelters or donate to charity. Clear out your home and prepare it for the long months ahead. Donate the items you clear out and be grateful for your bounty and the earth's sustenance.

Correspondences

Nature: Vegetables, apples, wheat, corn, mature roses

Symbols: An ear of corn, the scythe, and bread

Colors: Deep pink, gold, brown, amber, and red

Lammas Ritual

Lammas is the perfect time to try home baking, especially if you haven't done so before. Bake a simple loaf of bread and then place it on your altar. Break the bread into four quarters and place them at the points of the compass. Bless the bread and sprinkle it with water before sharing it with your family.

Mabon the Autumn Equinox 21st September

This is the final harvesting cycle when the last of the crops are brought in from the fields, and you begin to prepare for winter. The daylight hours are getting shorter, and the air is filled with a hint of frost. Mabon is the time to celebrate those last sunny days of summer and build fires to feast around. The leaves are falling, and it's time for you to shed some of your layers. Concentrate on self-doubt and how to get rid of it. Use magic to increase your self-confidence and love. Start a journal and make a wish list of things you will do in the following year.

Correspondences

Nature: Acorns, dried leaves, pine cones, horse chestnuts,

Symbols: Piles of harvested vegetables, leaves, the scythe, and bread

Colors: Red, orange, amber, brown, yellow, gold, and purple

Mabon Ritual

Cover your altar with a golden cloth and place two red candles on top. Use paper and pen to list the things you want to change about yourself. Light the candles and burn the paper safely as you ask the spirits to guide you. Watch the ashes fall to the floor and imagine your worst habits falling away from you. Extinguish the candle and thank the spirits for their attendance.

The wheel of the year may not be as important to our regular lives as it was for our ancestors, but it is a strong link to nature and the past. Perhaps it will alert you to the changing seasons and make you more in tune with how nature functions to bring food and sustenance to the table. Perhaps it will give you more reasons to connect with your friends and the spiritual world so you feel their energy and connection. It will remind you that cycles are part of life and that people need to flow with energy and be part of the wonder of nature.

Chapter 3: The Elements

There is a common belief that there are five fundamental elements in witchcraft and regular life, but this chapter includes an extra element that is often overlooked. The sixth element will bring increasing levels of power to your craft and will help you find different ways to use it in your work. In the popular game *World of Warcraft*, the power of the sixth element is apparent and forms part of weaponry – scientific studies use the element freely. What is this powerful element? Read on and discover exactly what you have been missing out on.

The 5 fundamental elements.
Jakub Jankiewicz (Jcubic), CC0, via Wikimedia Commons:
https://commons.wikimedia.org/wiki/File:Five_elements_and_pentagram.svg

The Six Elements and How to Invoke Them in Your Rituals

In witchcraft, many practitioners use the four cardinal points to bring power to their magic, and they call upon the four pillars to create a protective space and foundations to ensure their work is safe. The four pillars are Willingness, Knowing, Daring, and the Time of silence, but that's another branch of magic. The elements you are studying can be used alongside these strong foundations and pillars to create magical cohesive energy to fuel your spells and protect you as you work.

Many witches are familiar with the regular five elements. Still, the addition of the sixth will help you grow and become more effective, so let's explore the elements and how to bring them into your magical world.

Element: Air

Cardinal Direction: East

Corresponding Color: White or yellow

Pillar: Knowledge

The air brings energy through the slightest breeze or the most powerful gale. It moves seeds and pollen through the air to bring life to the earth. Air brings intelligence, speech, movement, and countless other strengths to your magic. Air is light and invisible, but it contains amazing strength and brings strength to spells for travel, knowledge, and finding what is lost. The element of air creates the image of cloudy skies. It represents mountain tops and windswept plains that inspire you to see the world.

Air spells are best performed in spring and include the use of wands and crystals like citrine. Use incense and smudge sticks to invoke the air element and appeal to the deities you follow to join you in your craft. Air deities include a modern figure from American folklore, Aradia, who appears in the popular 1899 work, The Gospel of Witches. Her name also connects to a powerful Italian goddess; she is a key figure to work with when using the element air in your spells.

Air Spells

The Creativity and Wind Magic Spell

This will help you release your inner creativity and increase your personal strength. It is an effective way to identify your strengths and weaknesses and allow for personal growth. This spell gives you an insight into your own form and lets you connect to the elements and feel their power.

What You Need:
- Freshly-cut spring flowers
- Wind instrument (anything will do, a penny whistle or a cheap recorder works just as well as expensive and ornate flutes)
- Freestanding yellow candle
- Sage smudge stick

Choose a place where you connect to nature and cleanse it with your sage. Seat yourself on the floor and place the candle in front of you. Light the candle and place your wind instrument between yourself and the candle.

Say the words,

"Yellow candle in the wind and air, bring creativity to share. Show me how to find my inner artist and bless my work with originality and love."

Visualize how this will manifest. Are you a painter or a writer? Do you want to do something physical like crafting or sculpting? If you are unsure, just close your eyes and let the element of air fill your lungs by breathing deeply and letting the air out slowly. Images should appear that help you identify what you are destined to achieve.

Pick up the instrument and play notes on it. Don't try and replicate a tune you already know. This is a spell for your creativity, not to celebrate someone else's work. Let the notes flow and float away on the wind as you hear the melody and bask in the sweetness and purity of the noise.

Imagine an instrument as a tool that draws in the energy of air and feel it fill your lungs with pure oxygen. Feel the energy fill you with hope and love and imagine your energy levels rising. Think back to the visualization and the creative activity you saw.

Set the instrument down, extinguish the candle, and thank the spirits and elements for their interactions before you leave. Go and begin the creative activity.

Smoke Air Travel Spell
What You Need:
- Feather
- A sprig of fresh mint
- Hand fan
- Small yellow bag

Crush the fresh mint by hand or using a pestle and mortar. Take a moment to breathe in the smell and let it fill your lungs and nose.

Take the feather in your hand and visualize where you want to travel to. Imagine the whole process, the packing, the journey, and eventually, arriving at your chosen destination. Throw the feather in the air and use the fan to keep it off the floor. Keep fanning until you feel the spell is finished, and catch the feather in your hand. Place the mint and the feather in the bag and carry it with you until you arrive at your chosen destination.

Element: Fire

Fire is a masculine element perfect for spells involving passion, sex, power, and strength.

Cardinal Point: South

Color: Red or orange

Solid Shape: Triangular

Pillar: Willfulness

Fire spells are mostly candle spells, but you can go bigger with burning rituals if you do them safely. Fire consumes and cleanses, and it is the source of food and water. It creates the fuel that fires humankind and gives light and heat to mankind. It brings drive and determination to your spells and ensures they will be more effective.

Fire spells are great for witchcraft newbies as they are impressive yet simple to perform. But it wasn't always so. Imagine your ancestors experiencing fire for the first time and the way it changed their lives. Now remember the phenomenon of wildfires and the terror they bring to the areas where they occur. Fire shouldn't be underestimated, and it should be respected and revered. When you use fire in your magic, it is simple to strike a match and produce instant flames but imagine how it feels to use flint and steel to create your elemental ingredient. Try and create fire with natural elements and feel the extra strength it brings to your magic.

Fire Banishment Spell

This spell is meant to get rid of the energies that are holding you back. Negativity from a past relationship or weaknesses you feel stop you from moving forward. Never use this spell to eliminate living objects or people; that is pushing the boundaries too far. If you have doubts about anything, this spell will clear them and give you the intuition to move forward and achieve your goals.

What You Need:

- Cauldron, this can be any size pot providing it is fireproof
- Paper and pencil
- BBQ starter gel
- Match or lighter

Take the paper and pencil and write a single word to represent what you want to banish. Is grief or sadness holding you back? Is doubt your anchor? Write the word clearly and with intent.

Fold the paper and place it in the cauldron. Add the flammable gel and light the match. Throw the match onto the gel and watch that initial burst of flame shoot up and light the room.

Say the words,

> *"Fire does burn the word so bright; it makes the issue leave my sight; no more will I have to fight; from this day forward, the world is right."*

Hold your hand over the cauldron when it is safe, and visualize what you want to banish. Imagine it as a solid form and see it disappear from the pot and float away from you. Now the spell is finished, and the energy has dispersed. Thank the spirits and the element for their help, and move on with your regular life.

Element: Water
Cardinal Direction: West
Color: Blue
Alchemic Symbol: Inverted triangle
Pillar: Daring

What do you think of when you hear the word water? Is it a cooling drink to quench your thirst or the hot water that cleanses you? Do you imagine the sea, amazing waves, and wildlife that populate the oceans? Maybe rivers and lakes or huge powerful waterfalls? Whatever you imagine, the power and strength of water is indisputable.

Water flows and changes to suit the vessel that holds it, and just one tiny drop can cause ripples that change the environment. Water is the grand force that creates canyons and gullies and is the element of our emotions. It represents the mysteries of life, and in magic, it is used to tap into the deepest secrets people hold beneath their cognizant selves. Use water to become more intuitive and allow yourself to become more malleable but retain your original form.

The beauty of the element water is its availability. Unlike fire, you don't have to create it, it is everywhere, and you choose which water is used. Start to connect to the element by appreciating it in all its forms. Raise your face to the skies as it rains and let cold snowdrops melt on you. Thank the elemental forces whenever you drink water or wash your hands.

The Water Protection Spell
What You Need:
- Water
- Sea salt
- Bowl. *(Don't use a kitchen bowl; use one that is solely for magic purposes to add intent and purity)*
- Fresh or dried mint or parsley

If you can, perform the spell near a body of natural water like a pond or lake. Create a circle of protection with your salt keeping some back for the spell. You can fortify the circle with eight stones to bring added protection.

Step into the circle and sit down with your supplies. Add the water, salt, and herbs, and start visualizing what you require from the spell. What do you want to protect? Your home, your family, yourself, or your partner? It can be anything that comes to mind. Imagine locking yourself in a small room with thick walls and solid doors that protect you. Now see yourself lying on the floor and surrounded by things that make you feel calm and at peace. This can be a litter of puppies or a warm blanket. The main thing is to feel protected. It doesn't matter about details; it's all about the sensation of feeling safe.

Now hold the bowl in front of you and gaze into the water. Let your fears flow into the water and be cleansed by salt and herbs.

Say the words,

> *"There is no cause for alarm; I am free from things that can harm; this water is my protection and will block evil before it has begun."*

Now feel the negativity entering the bowl and becoming part of the water. You can further cleanse the solution with regular iodized salt and leave the liquid for a few moments. Remove the herb without touching the tainted water and bury it in the ground and say the words:

> *"Dear sprig of herb, I thank you, Keep me free from harm and safe and free."*

The process can be repeated until you feel completely protected and safe from harm. When the spell is done, wash the bowl with clean, cold water and say a blessing over it before putting it away until next time.

Element: Earth

Cardinal Direction: North

Color: Black

Alchemic Shape: An inverted triangle with a line through the top section

Pillar: Silence

Earth is the base of nature. It represents solidity and tangible strength. Earth elements may seem less flashy than the others, but they are reliable and secure. Think of the amazing things that spring from the Earth; plants and flowers, foodstuff, and trees are all around you, but what else does the earth yield? Think about the diamonds and other Earth fortune-telling forms on the Earth.

Think of the Earth element as the Higgs Boson of your witchcraft; it brings the matter to your intent and makes it a tangible object. It is a healing element and works in spells that connect you to the essence of nature. Ancient civilizations created gardens and stone circles to channel the earth's energy (think Stonehenge or Machu Picchu) so you could create the same effect in your home.

The Earth Healing Mandala

Buddhists created mandalas to represent the universe – but in this example, you are creating a connection to the Earth. Choose a square box or garden planter and fill it with soil and sand. Choose a selection of white seeds and plant them in the corners to represent the four corners of creation. Now use a selection of colored seeds and grains to create a geometric pattern in the box. You can choose whatever pattern you like and whatever representation you desire. Be creative and energized, and fill the experience with joy.

You can chant and sing as you plant the seeds and maybe plant some in the moonlight to bring lunar energy. Let your inner voice guide you and show you the pattern in your mind. Once you have completed the mandala, leave it to root for seven days before you replant the seeds in your garden. The process can be repeated as many times as you like to spread the magic and bring the energy of Earth to your life.

Earth Protection Spell for the Home

Use Earth connections to make your home safe and free from attack by negative forces.

What You Need:

- 4 different dried herbs, cinnamon, black cohosh, tea, and cloves, work
- 4 black stones
- 4 natural pieces of wood, branches that have fallen, or driftwood

Bless all the items with the following words

"Mother Earth and sacred ground, here to stay, the magic is bound, to protect my home and keep it safe. Within these items, power is bound; by our reverence, our wounds will heal, and with these words, the magic is sealed."

Use the items to create a safe space around your home and form a barrier to all evil and negativity. You can repeat the words as many times as you like.

These are the traditional four elements of witchcraft and will help you become a more effective witch. The next two elements are less physical and more ethereal but are just as important in magic.

The Element of Self or Spirit

This element is non-physical and represents the connection between all things. It connects us to the universe and increases our awareness of the otherworldly magic.

It is represented by the colors white, violet, and black.

In magic, the crystal quartz brings the energy of spirit, and the number 1 is the corresponding number.

Its corresponding shape is a circle or spiral representing the power of the cycle of nature.

The fifth element isn't a modern concept. Aristotle and Plato began to debate the existence of a missing non-physical element, and they felt something was missing from the equation. They coined the element "*Aether*," which has become part of our language as "ether." The spirit element has no form and is pure energy, and invoking the spirit element is a powerful way to make your spells more potent.

How to Invoke the Spirit Element

Most practitioners use deities to invoke the spirit element, but others use spirit guides. There are six steps to invoking the element and summoning the energy to your world.

1. **Determine the spell or ritual you are going to perform.** The spirits need to know what energy to bring. Are you casting for love, financial gain, or protection? Be clear with your requirements and give as many details as you can. Setting your intention is crucial to success, so don't rush the process.
2. **Choose a spirit that suits your needs.** What energy does your spell need? Do you have connections to your spirit guides and ancestors? This topic will be covered later in the book, so you will better understand the available energy.
3. **Choose a time.** Timing is everything, and depending on your beliefs, you should plan to craft at a time when you feel most powerful and connected to the universe. If you work better with lunar energy, plan to craft at night. If you feel an affinity to certain astrological forces, check charts to choose an effective time for your work.
4. **Cleanse yourself.** This is an important part of the process. Use your regular cleansing ritual to dispel all the negative

energies and physical dirt from your body. Once you are cleansed, dress for the occasion in clean white clothes so your whole ethos sets your intention.

5. **Plan your words.** Write down your invocation and use positive and uplifting words. Say them clearly and with energy so the spirits know your intentions are true.

6. **Thank the spirits for their attention.** You should repeat the invocation as many times as needed, and you will know when the ritual has worked. After the intention is met, thank the spirits for their love and energy and meditate to regain your connection to the physical world.

And finally, the sixth element. Read on.

The Element of the Void

This element is the witchcraft version of the big bang theory. The dark void from which everything came. In magical terms, it is the starting pistol that signals the beginning of the race. It brings energy and intent to manifestation and acknowledges the power of the void.

There are several ways to bring the element of void to your craft. You can symbolize its presence with a black candle or an empty black vessel on your altar or directly invoke the element with a chant.

Chant to Invoke the Void

"I call upon the dark and formless part of the universe that gave birth to the eternal energy to bring itself to my work. I stand at the crossroads of magic and potentiality and ask that my words create success. As I speak, so may it be!"

These six elements are your keystones for witchcraft and will be there for you when needed. Remind yourself of their power by placing a pentagram close to your altar. The five points represent the first five elements, and the spaces remind you of the void.

Chapter 4: Gods and Goddesses in Witchcraft

Many witches choose to work with higher powers to assist them in their craft. They use these connections just like friendships in regular life and often have deities related to or associated with different religions and beliefs. Just like regular friendships, you need to understand the characteristics of these deities and how they work. With this knowledge, you can choose deities that suit your personality and beliefs – those which work with you at a pace that suits both of you. Choosing these deities and powers is as important as choosing the right tools or herbs to suit your magic.

Let's start with Wiccan deities. Wiccans are generally polytheists, meaning they worship more than one deity and invoke many gods and goddesses to bring them closer to the divine spirit of the universe. In Wiccan beliefs, the divine spirit is the very center of their magic, and all paths lead to this ultimate source.

The divine spirit is incomprehensible to human conception. Wiccans use deities to filter the divine spirit into traits and characteristics that we can understand. They all represent certain aspects of the spirit that help you form a bigger picture and better understand the divine spirit and what it means.

The Wiccan Triple Goddess

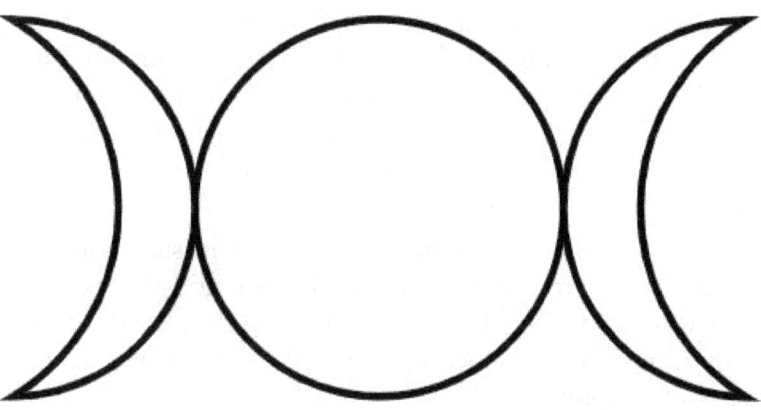

The symbol represents the three cycles of womanhood, the maiden, the mother, and the crone.
https://commons.wikimedia.org/wiki/File:Triple-Goddess-Waxing-Full-Waning-Symbol.svg

The symbol of the triple goddess is a full moon accompanied by the waxing and waning moon. The goddess has three separate identities, and they represent the three cycles of womanhood. The maiden, the mother, and the crone are the three representations of femininity.

The Maiden

The beautiful young woman who is just starting to live her adult life. She represents the opportunities of life and the start of new beginnings. Witches call upon the maiden in spells for purification and blessings.

The Mother

At this stage, the goddess has become the embodiment of womanhood, and she is the symbol of fertility and life. The goddess is called upon in rituals that bless children or promote fertility, and she is also called upon to give guidance and wisdom. Wiccans believe that this stage of the goddess is just as important as their real mother.

The Crone

In regular society, older ladies are often associated with frailty and weakness, but Wiccans believe otherwise. They recognize the importance of experience and wisdom and will call upon the crone to bring knowledge from the spiritual world. Wiccans believe that the crone is the height of her power, and she is the source of everlasting power and psychic development.

The Horned God

While the triple goddess is the feminine representation of Wicca, the male counterpart is the horned god. He is strongly connected to the underworld and is often invoked in funeral rites and communicating with the dead. The horned god has antlers and can seem scary and evil, but he is a benevolent deity who acts as a guide and protector. Death is a normal part of life, and Wiccans embrace this and use the horned god to guide them to the underworld.

Some people connect the horned god to the Christian concept of the devil, but this is a false connection. The horned god was worshiped by the Pagans way before the era of Christianity, and he predates the Devil by centuries. He is a protector, represents the omnipotent father figure, and is a power of nature.

The Wiccan Lord and Lady

Symbolized by the female aspect of the sun and the male energy of the moon, the lord and lady are representatives of the duality of nature. They symbolize how male and female energies combine to create magic. In Wiccan ceremonies, the high priest and priestess will often adopt the roles of the lord and lady.

The One

Technically not a deity, The One is more like a cosmic ocean where every living and spiritual thing originated. Wiccans believe that all life comes from The One and don't invoke it or worship it like a deity. Instead, they use the energy from The One to inspire their work and create more effective magic.

Gods and Goddesses for Witchcraft

Sometimes, choosing certain deities to work with can be challenging and overwhelming. There are so many religions and belief systems to choose from that it is difficult to know where to start. The list below will help you start the process and connect you to some of the more approachable deities used by witches and other magical practitioners.

Adonis and Aphrodite – The original power couple who are powerful Greek deities. They can help you with spells for love and passion, bringing purity to your spellcasting.

Adonis and Aphrodite.
https://commons.wikimedia.org/wiki/File:Venus_and_Adonis.jpg

Artemis and Apollo – Twin sister deities that work well in lunar magic.

Artemis and Apollo.
https://commons.wikimedia.org/wiki/File:Gavin_Hamilton_-_Apollo_and_Artemis,_1770.jpg

Athena – The Greek goddess of hunting brings strength and courage to your craft.

Athena, goddess of hunting.
https://commons.wikimedia.org/wiki/File:Theodoor_van_Thulden_-_Athena_and_Pegasus_(1654).jpg

Bast – The Egyptian goddess of cats and a source of feline wiles and knowledge.

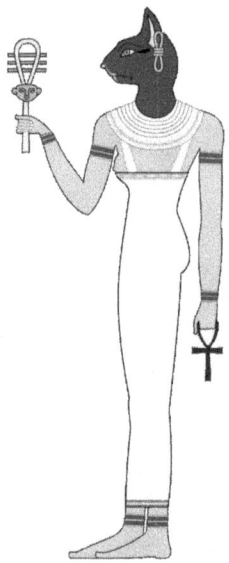

Bast, goddess of cats.
Gunawan Kartapranata, CC BY-SA 3.0 <https://creativecommons.org/licenses/by-sa/3.0>, via Wikimedia Commons: https://commons.wikimedia.org/wiki/File:Bastet.svg

Belenus or Bel – The Gaullist god of light and the sun, this Celtic god is often depicted with his horse and has powers related to equine strengths.

Bel, god of light and the sun.
https://commons.wikimedia.org/wiki/File:Marduk_and_pet.jpg

Brigid – The Celtic goddess of fertility and inspiration, invoked for fertility rites and the blessing of children.

Brigid, goddess of fertility and inspiration.
https://commons.wikimedia.org/wiki/File:Thecomingofbrideduncan1917.jpg

Cerridwen - Welsh goddess of the moon and harvest; she brings abundance and prosperity to magic.

Cerridwen, goddess of the moon and harvest.
https://commons.wikimedia.org/wiki/File:Ceridwen.jpg

Cernunnos - Celtic god of fertility and nature. He represents the underworld and is often pictured with horns and hooves.

Cybele - The Greek goddess of natural cavers who is especially effective in spells and rituals performed in nature, especially mountain tops and caves.

Demeter - The Greek goddess of fruitfulness. She brings good luck, prosperity, and abundance, especially to spells and rituals for crops and agriculture.

Diana - The Roman goddess of the hunt. Diana is a powerful female deity and brings courage, endeavor, and love to magic.

Dryads - A collection of tree spirits that are featured in Greek mythology. They are female representations of free spirit and playfulness. They bring lightness and joy to your magic.

Dryads.
https://commons.wikimedia.org/wiki/File:Tanz_der_Dryaden.jpg

Flora - The Roman goddess of spring. Her energy is often used in rebirth magic and spells for new beginnings. She is a young and vibrant goddess who is filled with love and joy.

Fortuna - The Roman goddess of fate. Invoke her when you are performing divination or want to see what the future holds for you. She is a benevolent spirit who will work with you to change your fate and improve your future.

Freya - Also known as Frigg, is the Norse goddess from Asatru belief who is the consort of Odin and the leader of the Valkyries. She rules as the Queen of Asgard and the foremost goddess of Norse beliefs.

Hathor - The Egyptian goddess of the sky. She is especially effective in magic that is performed by females. Her protective energy is used to keep women safe and brings fertility and safety to them. She is often portrayed as a female form with a cow's head.

Hera - The wife of Zeus, Hera is the Greek goddess of marriage and relationships. She is one of the most effective goddesses of Greek mythology and can be invoked to bring feminine energy.

Hestia – The Greek goddess of home and hearth. Invoke her when you perform spells and rituals in your home to protect you from invasive energies.

Inanna – The Sumerian goddess of Heaven and divine law. She is a powerful sexual force and is especially effective in matters of love and law.

Isis – The Egyptian equivalent of the triple goddess of Wicca. She has the same three stages as the triple goddess.

Janus – The Roman God of entrances and transitions. He is especially effective in spells for new beginnings and guarding your emotional balance.

Kali – The consort of Shiva and a powerful source of both destruction and creation. Invoke her to banish your enemies or to help you start new activities.

Kali, the consort of Shiva and a powerful source of both destruction and creation.
https://commons.wikimedia.org/wiki/File:Dakshina_Kali_-_19th-century.jpg

Mayet – The Egyptian goddess of justice, truth, and legal matters.

Morrigan – The Celtic equivalent of the triple goddess, strongly associated with death and war. She is depicted as a crow and has dark magical powers.

Muses – In Greek mythology, the Muses are goddesses of literature, science, and the arts. There are nine muses, and they can be invoked as a spiritual team to help your magic be more effective.

Nike – The Greek goddess of victory. Her power is effective to magic devoted to speed and success. She is often depicted with wings and is an effective symbol of art and sports.

Norns – In Norse mythology, the Norns are the sacred guardians of the tree of life, Yggdrasil, and they are effective protectors and control the fate of all human beings. They draw water from the well of creation to feed the sacred tree and are powerful female spiritual entities.

Norns: sacred guardians of the Tree of Life.
https://commons.wikimedia.org/wiki/File:Die_Nornen_Urd,_Werdanda,_Skuld,_unter_der_Welteiche_Yggdrasil_by_Ludwig_Burger.jpg

Nut - The Egyptian goddess of the skies and the mistress of protection. She is depicted on all fours covering the Earth and protecting humankind.

Persephone - The Greek goddess of the underworld. Invoke her to help you cope with grief and guide your loved ones to the afterlife.

Selene - The Greek goddess of the moon.

Venus - The Roman goddess of love who is especially powerful in spells for love, lust, passion, and relationships.

Vesta - The Roman goddess of fire, both domestic and ritualistic.

How to Invoke or Evoke the Gods and Goddesses

One common witchcraft question is about invoking and evoking deities. Because the words sound similar, some beginners think the two practices are interchangeable when, in reality, the opposite is true. When you start working with deities, you must be extra careful and understand exactly what you are working with.

Evoking is the practice of asking a deity to join you during a ritual or working spell so you can benefit from their wisdom or energy. Any involvement is external and cannot harm you. Evoking can be achieved by a simple question or offering. For instance,

> *"Hail Venus, I ask you to join my sacred circle tonight and be part of my ritual for love and passion; we bring you this goblet of wine to show our love and respect."*

Then you hope the goddess hears your plea and joins you for your spell.

Invoking is a form of voluntary possession where the deity will manifest through your human form. This is much more involved than hanging out with your favorite deities and should only be performed by experienced witches. While the possession is always temporary, it is a good idea for beginners to practice evoking before they jump straight into invoking.

The Commonsense Guide to Invoking Deities

Once you feel ready to work with the deities, it is important to understand what preparation you need to do. Don't try and work with more than four deities when you first start, you need to get to know them, and they need to get to know you as well. The point is to be respectful and honorable and to build a relationship between both parties, so choosing too many deities could be confusing.

Other Preparations to Carry Out Before Invoking a Deity

- **Research and study your chosen deity.** Understand the myths in which they feature and their characteristics and personalities. What are their strengths, and what will they bring to your life?
- **Find appropriate ways to welcome your deity.** What adornments should you use to welcome them to your space? Appropriate symbols and figures from their cultural beliefs.
- **Choose suitable offerings** and libations for your chosen deity.
- **What are their favored animals or sacred items** which feature in their myths?
- **Document and research** any spells or rituals that are personal to the deity.
- **Look within your psyche** and be honest about the connection you feel to the deity.

The last point is the most important one. You need to feel a real connection and desire to work with your chosen deity. Sacred beings aren't in the market for casual relationships, and they will not respond to a halfhearted *"Hi, how are you"* because they are busy. Are you choosing this particular deity for the right reasons or just because they are cool and popular? The sacred beings you are invoking are serious about what they do and will only reply to people who are on the same wavelength as them.

Another thing to remember is that they are in charge. You could end up in a call-waiting system if your deity is busy, waiting a long time for an answer – only to be told no. That is the way of the universe when it comes to new energies; you may have to try multiple times before you achieve connection.

Why would you do all that preparation? Ask yourself if you would randomly walk up to a stranger in the street and ask them for help. Would you knock on a stranger's door and ask them to be part of your life?

It's a bit rude, not to say downright dangerous, and it just wouldn't happen. Magic isn't careless; you shouldn't cut corners because the whole process could spiral out of control. Good intentions aren't enough; you need to be thorough and respectful of the powers you are dealing with.

Ritual to Invoke a God or Goddess

Now you are ready to start the process. You have your chosen deity, are sure about your intent, and are mentally and physically ready to connect. What do you do next?

First, you must cleanse yourself spiritually and physically. Take a ritual bath with cleansing herbs and sea salt and let yourself dry naturally, don't rush the process using towels. Meditate before you start the ritual and dress in simple white cotton clothes.

Now you must ask for protection. Ask the spirits to keep you safe, and imagine a bright white light surrounding you as you feel their love and warmth. Now your body is protected, it's time to make a sacred space for your invoking ritual and spell. Take 40 candles and place them in a circle all around you. Sit in the middle of the circle and say the following:

> *"As I appear before you, almighty spirit, I ask for the wisdom to understand you. Give me access to your realm and grant me a safe passage to the inner domain. I ask for permission to enter your plane and connect to my chosen deity."*

You will feel different when you are given access and immediately feel lighter and more incisive. You could start to see images from the spiritual realm and feel the air around you change. Once you have stepped over the threshold, your energy levels will soar, and you can start to look for the answers you seek.

The next part of the invocation is incredibly personal, and the only advice you need is to follow your instinct and become immersed in the experience. Use your sincerity and love for the deities to connect with them. No formal words cover this connection; the words you use will come to you and will originate from your desire and need for their assistance.

Once you have connected to the deities and spirits, it's time to end the ritual. Thank the deities and spirits for their time and assistance, and cooperation. Be grateful for the answers you have received, and don't worry if all your queries haven't been answered. This starts a lifelong relationship with the divine universe and the higher beings occupying it.

How to Cast an Invocation Spell

This is a spell that can be used to draw spirits, deities, gods, and goddesses. It opens the lines between you and the spirit world. Cast this spell on a Wednesday during a full or dark moon for the best results.

What You Need:
- An offering for the deity – use your research to find out what is appropriate
- Silver candle (white will do if you don't have a silver one)
- Sage smudge stick
- 1 cup of sea salt

Prepare for the spell just as you would for the ritual by bathing and dressing in white. Cast your protection circle in salt and call the cardinal quarters for added protection. Light the smudge stick and use it to cleanse the area and yourself, then leave it burning in the circle. Take the candle and a holder and place them in the center of the circle while surrounding it with the gifts you have for the deity. Close your eyes and breathe deeply before you say the following:

"I call on you (insert deity name) and wait for you with an open mind and a grateful heart,

(Deities name) I call on you with an open mind and willing spirit,

(Deities name) I offer these gifts to honor you and make you feel welcome in my world,

Visit me and share your wisdom and knowledge and guide me through my craft."

When you feel the spell has finished, thank the deity for their attention and let the candle burn away naturally. Over the next few days, you will feel the sense of the deity's energy in your body, and you will hear voices and see images that originate from the deity's energy.

The bottom line is to trust your instincts and follow the path you are shown. Your regular senses are redundant in magic, and you need to call on your gut reaction and believe what you are being told. Use your mind and emotions to guide you and give yourself to the process.

Chapter 5: Tarot Cards

Tarot cards are a path to revealing the lessons of life.
https://unsplash.com/photos/fzMgicYhJws

In the past, tarot cards were dismissed as hokey, and the image of a dodgy fortune teller earning money from saps who wanted to know what their future held was a popular misconception. Today users know better. The tarot card readings are so much more than divination and fortune-telling over-represent, respectively. They are a map of your soul and a way to see the story of your life. Some people see tarot as images on a deck of cards with defined meanings and as just a bit of fun. True believers know it is a path to revealing the lessons of life and a key to tapping into universal wisdom to gain knowledge.

Tarot is a powerful tool to expand your consciousness and become more self-aware. Ask questions and get answers that reflect the wisdom of the universe intertwined with your powerful consciousness.

A Brief History of Tarot

The oldest tarot cards are believed to have been used in 1440 AD and were created for the Duke of Milan. It is thought they were originally used to play a game rather than tell fortunes, and they were hand painted and ornate.

The game quickly spread to the rest of Europe and became a staple of rich households. This continued for the next 300 years when occult practitioners used them as a divination tool. The images were linked to ancient Egyptian lore, astrology, and alternative illustrated cards. The deck developed into the tarot cards known today in the 1970s when a growing interest in psychoanalysis linked the cards' meanings to science.

The New Age movement of the 1970s meant that popular culture and beliefs spread the use of tarot, and the interest grew. Today there are thousands of decks to choose from, and tarot is becoming a primary way to meditate and reflect on your personal state of being. The cards can be used to create a life plan to what you already know and what the cards can tell you.

How to Choose Your First Tarot Deck

First, let's get rid of the biggest misconception about tarot decks. There is a superstition that your first deck should never be bought by yourself; instead, it should be a gift from someone else. This is rubbish and an old wife's tale. Getting your first deck is exciting, but it can be overwhelming. There are so many decks to choose from, so here are some tips to help you get started on your journey.

- Explore the imagery of the decks and use your gut feeling to guide you.
- Remember to choose your deck depending on your experience level; beginners' cards are easier to use and can ease you into the process.

- Do you want to use traditional or more modern decks?
- Where are you going to use the cards?
- Is the size appropriate and practical?
- Choose a quality deck depending on your budget.

If you are eager to get started, printable decks are available online. These give you a chance to start your tarot journey in minutes.

Familiarize Yourself with the Deck

All decks have 78 cards, and these are divided into 2 major groups.

The Major Arcana has 22 cards, starting with the Fool tarot card, number 0, and running through to the World tarot card, numbered 21. They work together to form a story known as the Fool's Journey, during which lessons can be learned from each archetype within the Major Arcana.

The Minor Arcana contains the rest of the cards and contain 4 suits of 14 cards each. These are the Cups, the Pentacles, Swords, and Wands.

The Suit of Cups

All the cards in this suit are related to the element of water and are related to matters of the heart. Cards from this suit show emotional connections and how you are dealing with your environment.

The Suit of Pentacles

All the cards in this suit relate to the earth element. These are also known as money cards and deal with your prosperity and achievements. They answer questions regarding your career, money-related decisions, and financial matters. It is just as important to get answers to material-based questions as it is to deal with emotional matters.

The Suit of Swords

All the cards in this suit relate to the element of air. These cards tell you about communication and action. The cards will appear in a reading when you need to be reminded to use your head rather than your heart. If you receive a card of Swords, you should pay attention to your environment and beware of conflict and arguments that are brewing beneath the surface.

The Suit of Wands

These cards are related to the element of fire. They represent passion and inspiration and indicate the need to get creative and start new projects. These cards add heat to your life and bring a burst of energy that inspires you to do better. They encourage you to examine your core beliefs and to follow a path that suits your need. Wand cards aren't passive. They are firecrackers that are designed to light your internal fires.

This is just the start of your understanding of tarot and what the cards are trying to tell you. The information above is like a basic alphabet, and learning tarot is just like learning a new language. All the cards have multiple meanings, and the meanings change depending on the other cards in a spread. Each card represents individual words, and when used together, they begin to form sentences. It's just like when you begin to speak a new language, and you start to recognize the nuances and inflections that can influence the meaning and change the mood of the message.

How to Understand Your Deck

As a beginner, it is tempting to choose multi-card spreads, but that is not the right way to start understanding your cards. Beginners need to learn how to walk before they can run, and this involves pulling a single card daily and following the steps below:

1. Think of your question. What is the main thing bothering you, or do you have a practical question you need to answer?
2. Close your eyes and visualize your question, how the different answers can manifest, and what can happen with multiple outcomes.
3. Open your eyes and pull a card from your deck.
4. Study the card at length.

Which card did you get, and from which part of the deck did it come? Use the information above to get the basic meaning of your card.

Study the imagery and look beyond the picture to see any hidden meaning. Are there any other cards you would like to see alongside your card? What would it mean in a conventional spread? If you pull your card in the morning, carry it with you for the rest of the day so you can feel its presence. Take the card out, study it whenever possible, and see if your feelings change as the day progresses.

At night, sleep with the card under your pillow and see what dreams you have. Are they related to the card and your perceived meanings, or are they completely different? Are your dreams telling you to change your perception, or are they confirming your initial thoughts? The following day you should start seeing signs related to the card and connecting the message. Over time you will realize that these things aren't happening by coincidence.

Repeat the process until you feel you have a deeper understanding of the deck and what the cards mean. You will instinctively know when to start using spreads instead of single cards and let the cards work to create stories for you.

Popular Spreads for Beginners and Advanced Users

You already know that tarot is based on instincts, but it is also influenced by the data you receive and how it is obtained. Choosing a pattern to represent your spread is the first step to triggering the process. This chapter deals with readings for yourself rather than other people, as this is the classic way to start your journey. You should never do readings for anyone else until you feel you have reached an expert level.

The Classic Three-Card Spread

You are both the reader and the querent in this reading, so you pose and answer the questions. The most common three-card spread involves the past, the present, and the future and begins with the first card setting the intent and theme of the answer that is being indicated.

The second card sets the nature of the question and the current position of your emotions or practical situation. It is placed alongside the first card before the third is pulled. This third card suggests the likely outcome and what the future looks like.

Once the three cards are in place, use your intuition to decipher the meaning and what your question is really about.

The Mind, Body, and Spirit three-card spread does the same as the past, present, and future spread but is more focused on adding balance to a reading. The first card represents the current state, the second is the approaching energies, and the third is advice for each realm.

The Five-Card Spread

This extends the three-card spread to include even more information and adds extra levels to the answers you can find. Five card tarot spreads help you get to the heart of the matter.

The spread should form a cross with the three original past, present and future cards forming the crosspiece. The other two cards are placed by the side to form the cross. The central three cards show the potential, while the additional cards indicate the brightest and darkest possibilities of the situation.

The Rectangle

Pull the first card from the deck and place it on the table. This is the theme card for the other four to relate to. Place it at the center and pull four additional cards to form a rectangle around the main card. The four cards represent the tools to be used, a lesson to be learned, another person's perspective, and any potential conflict or fears.

The Celtic Cross Spread

This spread uses ten cards and is an extension of the five-card spread. The first card represents your role in the question, and the second card is an obstacle you will face to reveal the answer. The second card crosses the first one and forms the center of the cross.

The third cross represents the foundation of the question that lies in the past. The fourth card is placed on the left side of the cross and represents an event that is happening in the present that is affecting the issue.

The fifth card is drawn and placed above the cross to represent the potential for success and a favorable outcome, while the sixth is something that will happen in the future that will bring about an outcome.

Once the cross has been formed, it's time to add four extra cards representing four more pieces of information that help address the issue.

Card 7 is related to past experiences and attitudes that may be affecting the theme of the question.

Card 8 is about external forces and their influence on the issue. Are there negative energies at work, or could the people around you make a difference in how you handle the issue?

Card 9 represents what your fears and hopes are. They will show you your subconscious feelings about issues, some of which have been hidden from sight.

Card 10 represents the probable outcome. It gives you the chance to accept your fate or do something to change it.

This is quite an advanced spread and can be confusing for beginners. Just like any other skill or gift, the more you practice, the better you will become. Just like learning a new language, tarot reading is an everlasting process, and you will learn more every time you use them.

FAQs about Tarot

Q1. Do I need to be psychic to read tarot cards?

No. You need to learn to trust your intuition and interpretation of the cards to guide you and read effectively. Of course, some people will have natural psychic abilities, which means that they are more effective than others, but it isn't essential to be psychic to read the cards.

Q2. Can anyone learn how to read tarot?

Yes, they can. Like the question above and just like regular life, some people will be more in tune with the cards and will have a natural affinity with them, but with practice and dedication, anyone can learn to read the cards.

Q3. Do you need intuition to read tarot cards?

Some people rely on their cards to give them a clear reading purely from the spread and the questions they are answering. This can lead to a dry reading without any wiggle room, but if you factor in intuition, you get a more effective and reliable reading that gives you a deeper connection to the cards.

Q4. Is my intuition fallible?

Just like all your instincts, intuition can lead you astray and down the wrong path. Even expert readers can be fooled by the signs and symbols the cards are showing and give the wrong reading. It's important to know that even though your intuition is critical for your readings, it isn't infallible and may be wrong.

Q5. Can tarot cards be used for fortune-telling?

No. They offer guidance and insight, but they should never be relied on to give you advice that changes your life. If you need professional advice, then seek it out. It's okay to ask the tarot cards for their take on things but always trust the professionals in certain matters. The cards can give you an insight into the future and the influences at play, but they aren't a predictive tool.

Tarot can be an exciting and powerful way to use your intuition to work with magic. It is a truly magical way to connect to the universe and your inner self. This is just a quick look at tarot, and if you feel a connection to the cards, you could be starting a lifelong relationship with your deck.

Chapter 6: Runic Divination

Runic symbols are believed to hold the keys to knowledge, wisdom, and spiritual power.
https://www.pexels.com/photo/runic-letters-on-wood-chunks-and-ground-with-autumn-leaves-10110445/

Norse and Germanic folklore were filled with magic and witchcraft, and the existence of runes and their divination powers are rooted in their history. The Elder Futhark runes are the most famous runes from history, and they originated in the 2nd century and were used for six centuries after. The alphabet was 24 characters long and was often carved into stones and wooden tiles. As with most languages and forms of communication, the alphabet was subject to change, and by the 8th century, it had been whittled down to a 16-character form of runes known as the Younger Futhark runes.

The runes were used as a form of writing, and Norse people would use them to create texts, but the gods and the Norns (the Norse fates) believed they were more magical than that and used them to write on Yggdrasil, the Norse tree of life. They were used to tell tales of the destinies of men and the powers of the gods and were considered magical and powerful ways to tell the future.

Odin taught the Norse people how to use the runes to practice divination and use magical symbols to protect their homes and weapons. Swords and shields from the Norse era would have runes engraved on them to ensure the Viking warrior who carried them would be safe. The use of magical symbols was widespread and began to include more symbols from mythology, like the Norse Compass and the Helm of Awe, but the main decorations were based on the runes.

The practice of divination with runes isn't clear because of the lack of written evidence, and most of the information about runic use is gathered from the Roman historian Tacitus who wrote about Viking life. It is believed that the runes would be carved on small objects like bones and sticks, and the runemaster would then use them to cast a reading. Most of the evidence suggests that runemasters would often be women, and they were regarded as the wise keepers of the runes. They would ask a question and then cast the runes onto a sacred space to gain an insight into the future, depending on where the runes fell. However, because of the lack of evidence, that is all that is known about the practice.

Modern Runic Divination

The advance of Christianity and the Latin language meant that runes were assigned to history for a long time. They were used by some isolated Scandinavian communities and are still used by them today. The re-emergence of runic magic began in the 17th century when a Swedish mystic associated with the emerging Kabbalah Jewish tradition was inspired to use runes for divination purposes. He was visited by spirits who sent him visions to inspire the use of the Younger Futhark runes in practice.

Some modern runemasters still use the Futhark runes, but the majority have adopted the Armanen runes created at the beginning of the 1900s by the Austrian occultist Guido von List. He based his runes on the earlier symbols. Still, over the last hundred years, they have also been adapted and changed to suit modern language. The symbols and their meanings must reflect matters of the era, so the more modern interpretations account for this.

Meanings of Runes

As already discussed, the meanings have their roots in Norse mythology and have been changed to suit modern needs. Still, many runemasters will incorporate both in their readings. Like tarot, runes have multiple interpretations based on how they fall and which other runes accompany them. The practice is based on intuition and what you see in the runes, but the meanings below will help you learn how to read the runes and adapt your thinking.

The table below lists the runes with their English phonetic form, how to pronounce them, and the meaning of the rune:

F - Frey - Wealth and riches

Frey, represents wealth and riches.
https://commons.wikimedia.org/wiki/File:Black_Rune_5.svg

U - Ur - Rain, snow precipitation

Ur, represents rain, snow, and precipitation.
Ekirahardian, OFL <http://scripts.sil.org/cms/scripts/page.php?item_id=OFL_web>, via Wikimedia Commons: https://commons.wikimedia.org/wiki/File:RUNIC_LETTER_URUZ_UR_U.svg

Th - Thur - Giant, dangerous, emotional distress

Thur, represents giant, dangerous, and emotional distress.
https://commons.wikimedia.org/wiki/File:Runic_letter_thurisaz.png

A - As - The Morse God Odin, wetlands, the kingdom of heaven

As represents the Norse god Odin, wetlands, and the kingdom of heaven.
File:B_rune_short-twig.png: User:Skadinaujovectorization:Own work, Public domain, via Wikimedia Commons: https://commons.wikimedia.org/wiki/File:B_rune_short-twig.svg

R - Reed - Ride, speed, travel, journey

200-450 AD   450-550 AD   550-750 AD

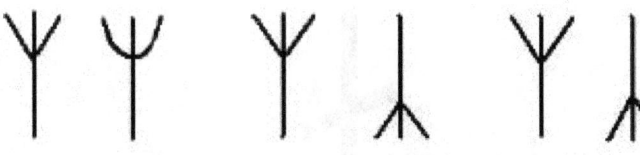

Reed, represents a ride, speed, travel, and journey.
Original uploader Berig, GFDL <http://www.gnu.org/copyleft/fdl.html>, via Wikimedia Commons: https://commons.wikimedia.org/wiki/File:R-runes.png

K - Kan - Death, illness, cancer, abscess

Kan represents death and illness.
Ekirahardian, OFL <http://scripts.sil.org/cms/scripts/page.php?item_id=OFL_web>, via Wikimedia Commons: https://commons.wikimedia.org/wiki/File:RUNIC_LETTER_K.svg

H - Hagal - Passageways, frost, cold

Hagal represents the cold.
Ekirahardian, OFL <http://scripts.sil.org/cms/scripts/page.php?item_id=OFL_web>, via Wikimedia Commons: https://commons.wikimedia.org/wiki/File:RUNIC_LETTER_HAEGL_H.svg

N - Naudr - Desire, need, barriers, obstacles

Naudr represents desire, need, barriers, and obstacles.
https://commons.wikimedia.org/wiki/File:Runic_letter_naudiz.png

I – Isa – Icicles, destruction, extreme cold

Isa represents icicles, destruction, and extreme cold.
Ekirahardian, OFL <http://scripts.sil.org/cms/scripts/page.php?item_id=OFL_web>, via Wikimedia Commons:
https://commons.wikimedia.org/wiki/File:RUNIC_LETTER_ISAZ_IS_ISS_I.svg

A – Arr – Abundance, harvesting, times of plenty

Arr represents abundance.
Osado, Public domain, via Wikimedia Commons:
https://commons.wikimedia.org/wiki/File:Runic_letter_ar.svg

S – Sol – Solar energy, sun, warmth, heat

Sol represents solar energy, sun, warmth, and heat.
Haisollokopas, CC BY-SA 4.0 <https://creativecommons.org/licenses/by-sa/4.0>, via Wikimedia Commons: https://commons.wikimedia.org/wiki/File:Sowilo_(alternate).svg

T - Tur - Justice, law, fairness

Tur represents justice, law, and fairness.
This W3C-unspecified vector image was created with Inkscape by Bloodofox and Stannered. W3C-validity not checked., Public domain, via Wikimedia Commons:
https://commons.wikimedia.org/wiki/File:Tiwaz_rune.svg

B - Bjork - New beginnings, springtime, the birch tree

Bjork represents new beginnings, springtime, and the birch tree.
Ekirahardian, OFL <http://scripts.sil.org/cms/scripts/page.php?item_id=OFL_web>, via Wikimedia Commons:
https://commons.wikimedia.org/wiki/File:RUNIC_LETTER_BERKANAN_BEORC_BJARKAN_B.svg

M - Madur - Humankind, man, male energy

Madur represents humankind, man, and male energy.
Ekirahardian, OFL <http://scripts.sil.org/cms/scripts/page.php?item_id=OFL_web>, via Wikimedia Commons: https://commons.wikimedia.org/wiki/File:RUNIC_LETTER_MANNAZ_MAN_M.svg

I - Logur - Liquids, water, nature, waterfalls

Logur represents liquids, water, nature, and waterfalls.
Ekirahardian, OFL <http://scripts.sil.org/cms/scripts/page.php?item_id=OFL_web>, via Wikimedia Commons:
https://commons.wikimedia.org/wiki/File:RUNIC_LETTER_LAUKAZ_LAGU_LOGR_L.svg

R - Yur - The yew tree, strength, tolerance, stamina

Yur represents the yew tree, strength, tolerance, and stamina.
Ekirahardian, OFL <http://scripts.sil.org/cms/scripts/page.php?item_id=OFL_web>, via Wikimedia Commons:
https://commons.wikimedia.org/wiki/File:RUNIC_LETTER_RAIDO_RAD_REID_R.svg

Do You Believe in Divination?

Back in Viking times, it was hard to conceive how many people believed in the process and how many believed in fate. Nordic folklore is filled with choices, and Asatru's religion is unique because *their gods were not worshiped*. Asatru followers believed their deities were prone to human frailties and would make mistakes just as humans do. The stories of the gods and goddesses are filled with incidents of them being tricked and fooled by mortals and other lesser beings.

It is important to recognize how modern rune readings work and what they can and can't tell you. Casting these magical symbols is fun and a great way to connect to magic, but it should never replace common sense and professional advice. Don't use reading to make life-changing decisions based on their answers. Instead, you should use the runes to help you get a better insight into what your subconscious is telling you and what the universe is suggesting. They are used to create a "divine spark" that connects you to the power of your mind, how you form an intrinsic part of the universe, and how everyone has a part to play. The difference between tarot and runes is the material used to create the runes. Tarot is highly personalized, while runes are made from physical materials that are part of the universe, like stones, glass, wood, and rocks.

Runes will often hint at an answer and show you the way to pursue the hints. The actual meaning of the word is whisper, secret, or mystery, depending on what you read. If your questions have multiple layers and need deeper introspection, then runes may be more effective than tarot, but the choice is yours. In Wiccan practices, runes are used to protect as well as to connect to the spiritual realm so you feel safer in your practices.

How to Choose Your Runes

Just like tarot decks, there are a lot of different rune sets to consider. There are ornate sets using materials like glass, crystal, and metal, and many simple sets are made from wood or stones. The material is your choice, and you may want to start with something simple to begin with. If you are naturally crafty, then consider making your own set from pebbles or wood. This way, you can start to feel a connection immediately, and your runes will be charged with your energy.

How to Store Your Runes

If you buy your runes, they will often come with a handy drawstring bag to keep them clean and safe. If you have made your own runes, you can buy pouches to store them or create a bag that suits your runes. They can also be kept in a box decorated with symbols and magical signs to keep their energy pure.

A rune cloth can be used to polish your set and keep it free from dust and negative energy. As a beginner, it can be a simple duster or a white cotton handkerchief, but as you start to form a relationship with your runes, you may want to choose something more personal. The cloth you choose can also be a base for your casting and create a boundary to keep negative energy out.

How to Get Started with Rune Casting

Choose a spot to cast that is familiar and brings you joy and peace. You must feel safe and relaxed, or your reading will be affected by stress. Take ten minutes to clear your mind and get rid of the detritus of regular life. Once you feel relaxed and ready to start, lay your rune cloth or board on the floor and start to think about the question you are asking. If you have connections with higher energies, call upon them to join you and guide your reading.

Just as with tarot, you should start with single runes to acquaint yourself with the set. Place your hand in the bag, draw your rune, and place it on the cloth or board. What does it say to you? What does it mean regarding your question? Focus on the single rune and what it is telling you.

Classic Rune Layouts and Casts

The Three Rune Layout

This simple cast is perfect for beginners and will help you start your journey with the runes. Reach into your bag and take the first rune out. Place it on your cloth or board with intent. This first rune should be right of center. Now draw the second rune and place it in the center before drawing the third to go to the left.

Rune 1 - This represents the overview of your situation or question. It is the rune's general opinion about what is happening and will help to set the scene.

Rune 2 - This represents the challenge and obstacles that lay before you.

Rune 3 - This represents the course of action and what you can do to get past these obstacles and be successful.

The Five Rune Layout

This extension of the three-rune layout includes more specific time periods. The first rune should be laid at the center of the cloth, while the four remaining runes form a cross around it. Rune 2 should be at the west point, 3 should be at the north, 4 at the south, and 5 should be at the east.

In this reading, the runes should be placed face down and turned over in order of placing to give a more effective reading. The horizontal runes 2, 1, and 5 represent the past, the present, and the future, while rune 4 represents the elements of the problem, and rune 3 relates to what you need to do to resolve the issue.

The Nine Rune Cast

This is for more experienced casters but gives you a more detailed and insightful answer to your questions. When using this casting method, you must fully delve into your spiritual learnings and prepare for the experience. You may want to directly connect to your spirit guides and ask for their guidance before you cast and ask them to join you in your reading. You can enhance your surroundings with magical tools and a candle or two. Dress for the occasion in simple white robes to make the reading feel more magical.

Of course, you can just cast your runes as normal in a quiet place that connects you to the universe. Divination is more achievable when you feel relaxed and comfortable, so your surroundings should reflect that. Some people may be more at home in a loud environment, while others prefer naturally calm surroundings. We are all different, and magic helps us celebrate that fact.

Reach into your bag and select nine runes at random. If your runes are large, then use both hands to choose them and then hold onto the runes for a moment or two. Now scatter the runes on your cloth or board while you look upwards. Consider the runes and how they have fallen. The ones near the center are considered the most important, while those on the periphery are less influential. If the runes are touching or very close, they could be complimentary runes that strengthen their influence. If the runes are face down, they should be left that way while you study the ones that have landed face up. Take a notebook and make a note of them so you can study them later before you turn over the remaining runes. Remember to place the runes you have turned over in exactly the same position they landed in so you get the overall picture when all nine runes are in place. The runes you have turned over represent the future and other outside influences that could affect your issues. They also represent the potential of new possibilities and future opportunities.

The Three Norns Cast

This is another simple cast based on the Norse divinities known as the Norns. The three principle Norns were sisters who lived beside the Well of Ur and created the fate of mankind. This rune cast represents the sisters and helps you see different aspects of your issue.

The first rune should be cast to represent the past and how it affects you. Do you have issues from your past that have followed you into your current life and are affecting you? The rune will highlight any historical issues.

The second rune gives you a deeper understanding of your issues and how they affect you.

The third rune is attuned to the future and will show you how to move forward.

There are hundreds of different casting layouts and ways to use the runes. Once again, you should use your intuition to guide you to the layouts that work for you.

Casting Boards

Some practitioners prefer to use a board decorated with Nordic symbols to bring further depth to their casts. These boards are similar to Ouija boards in some cases, with letters and numbers on them and a dedicated *Yes* and *No* area. Other boards concentrate on Nordic symbols like the Norse cosmos, which can represent the different areas of the Nordic universe. The central realm of Midgard represents the heart of the reading, while the inner realms of Asgard and Helheim represent the psychological influences. The outer realms of Jotunheim and Muspelheim are the unprejudiced areas of the universe.

The elements can also create a powerful runic board. Choose a board and divide it into four equal sections. Paint or color the sections white, red, blue, and green to represent respectively air, fire, water, and earth. Draw a magic circle in the center and decorate it with your favorite symbols and signs. When you want a detailed cast, simply scatter the whole bag of runes onto the board.

How each rune falls will tell you something different. Are they in the circle or outside? What color are they in, or do they land on the dividing line? What do the elements mean to you?

Air

Generally, air represents intelligence and creativity. It is the element of new beginnings, and if your rune falls in this section, it relates to your intangible issues and how to deal with them. This is the element of creativity and moving forward.

Fire

The element of passion and love fire can mean removing impurities and stopping harmful habits. Are there things holding you back? Burn them and move on. Fire is the symbol of transformation, and your rune will land there to signify your inner strength and the heat of your passion.

Water

Emotional and unconscious issues will be dealt with in this section. Water is one of the two physical elements and represents the ability to change and interact. Water fills spaces with ease and is considered a natural signal to become more adaptable and accept your situation.

Earth

The second physical element is less fluid than water and represents stability and foundation. Earth symbolizes fertility and material objects, and your rune will highlight what new beginnings you need to address. It is the element of stillness and endings, so your rune could tell you what part of your life has ended and how to move on.

The circle on the board could represent the other element we covered earlier, the element of spirit. If your rune falls within the circle, it could mean it is more personal and related to yourself, while outside the circle could mean it represents your environment.

Your runes and boards should represent your personality and beliefs. If you feel inspired by Disney characters or figures for literature, then use them to decorate your boards. There are no hard and fast rules to runic divination;. Your inspiration should be how you fuel your intuition, so be creative and create multiple sets to suit the situation. Runes and runic boards are by nature decorative, so use them to decorate your home or sacred space to bring color and protection.

Chapter 7: Crystal Divination

Crystals represent some of nature's most beautiful aspects in their greatness.
https://unsplash.com/photos/g95sf8-fEQg

When you think of crystal divination, most people think of the crystal ball, a mystical gypsy woman in a booth at the fair, and tales about what will happen. Modern witches know that divination is all about connecting to your inner psyche and the universe, and they understand that one of the most effective materials to use is crystals. They are naturally incredible and represent some of nature's most beautiful aspects in their magnificence.

Crystals are powerful and beautiful, and your collection will clearly indicate how you work and connect to the universe. Have you ever noticed how some people look like their pets? Well, choosing a crystal is a bit like choosing a puppy. You should feel an immediate connection with it and be prepared to look after it, nurture it, and care for it as you would a child or pet.

Crystals to Enhance Divination

This list contains just a few suggestions and will help you choose your starter kit for divination purposes.

Apophyllite - This crystal is the keeper of the Akashic Records, the knowledge of what all lives will look like and what happens to each of us. This crystal helps you break the barrier between the physical and spiritual worlds and keeps the physical body safe during your astral travels. Use the apophyllite to help you with out-of-body experiences and astral traveling.

Apophyllite brings down the barrier between the physical and spiritual worlds.
*Rob Lavinsky, iRocks.com - CC-BY-SA-3.0, CC BY-SA 3.0
<https://creativecommons.org/licenses/by-sa/3.0>, via Wikimedia Commons:
https://commons.wikimedia.org/wiki/File:Apophyllite-54502.jpg*

Amethyst – The third eye crystal and the representative of the crown and heart chakras. Because amethyst is so in tune with your higher chakras, it is the perfect choice for divination pendulums. Suspend the crystal from a chain and ask it questions with an answer board or by using left and right to indicate yes and no.

Aquamarine – A healthy clarifying stone, aquamarines are connected to the element water. They will help you focus and become more in tune with your psychic abilities.

Azurite – A crystal attuned with extremely high frequencies and gives you the power to enhance your third eye and higher crown chakras. Azurite is also used to make crystal elixirs for physical healing and energy readings. Soak the crystal in water to create an elixir to drink before you do tarot readings or crystal gazing so you increase your intuition and clairvoyance.

Azurite can improve your clairvoyance.
Ivar Leidus, CC BY-SA 4.0 <https://creativecommons.org/licenses/by-sa/4.0>, via Wikimedia Commons: https://commons.wikimedia.org/wiki/File:Azurite_-_New_Nevada_Lode,_La_Sal,_Utah,_USA.jpg

Beryl – Golden beryl is a highly effective stone for scrying and other magic rituals.

Bloodstone – This crystal facilitates your clairaudience powers so you can hear the spirits clearly and understand their message. It also enhances dreaming and can make your nightly messages more distinct and direct.

Calcite – The crystal of astral traveling and out-of-body experience. Use it when you want to cross the veil and channel your higher purpose. Spirits connect to calcite and will use their energy to bring clearer and more detailed messages.

Calcite can help with out-of-body experiences.
Rob Lavinsky, iRocks.com – CC-BY-SA-3.0, CC BY-SA 3.0
<*https://creativecommons.org/licenses/by-sa/3.0*>, *via Wikimedia Commons:*
https://commons.wikimedia.org/wiki/File:Calcite-20188.jpg

Carnelian – Aids clairvoyance and helps the living transition to the spirit world. Use it in divination spells to connect with your ancestors and receive their messages. Carnelian enhances your psychic abilities and develops your connections to your guides.

Celestite – Helps when you need to recall a dream that feels important but has become vague in your waking mind. Improves communication with the spiritual world and the higher energies.

Fluorite – The purple or violet form of fluorite improves your psychic connections and helps you decipher psychic messages. Use it in spells and rituals to get a clearer idea of what the spirits are trying to tell you.

Herkimer Diamond – Helps the user connect to spirit guides and collect information about their past lives. Aids clairvoyance and other psychic strengths.

Herkimer diamonds can help you connect to spirit guides.
Didier Descouens, CC BY-SA 4.0 <https://creativecommons.org/licenses/by-sa/4.0>, via Wikimedia Commons: https://commons.wikimedia.org/wiki/File:Herkimer.jpg

Iolite – Strengthens psychic abilities and can help users find their psychic on-button and activate their spiritual connections.

Jasper – Increases the quality of dreams and adds prophetic skills so the user can interpret signs and symbols from the spirit world.

Jasper increases the quality of dreams.
Linas Juozėnas, CC BY-SA 4.0 <https://creativecommons.org/licenses/by-sa/4.0>, via Wikimedia Commons: https://commons.wikimedia.org/wiki/File:Picture-jasper.jpg

Labradorite – If you want a starter stone to use in divination, choose this one. According to Eskimo legend, the famous natural phenomenon, the Northern Lights, were once trapped in rocks along the Canadian coast at a place called Labrador. A famous warrior was traveling in the region and recognized what was happening. He used his mystical spear to free the lights and restore them to the heavens. Because the lights had been trapped for so long, they left a beautiful mark on the stones, and these became the powerful crystal labradorite we know today. They are the most powerful stones for divination and will help all your senses and connections.

Lapis Lazuli – An important stone for protection and spiritual enhancement. It enhances your third eye chakra and brings increased psychic communication.

Lapis Lazuli is helpful for protection.
Adam Ognisty, CC BY-SA 3.0 <https://creativecommons.org/licenses/by-sa/3.0>, via Wikimedia Commons: https://commons.wikimedia.org/wiki/File:2_lapis_lazuli.jpg

Malachite – This crystal works as an effective partner for azurite; together, the crystals give extra strength and psychic intuition.

Merlinite – Aids traveling through past lives and gaining extra knowledge from former existences. Helps the user to find knowledge to help them become more ascended and developed.

Moonstone – Links the user to lunar energy and helps them to achieve heightened spiritual connections. Enhances lucid dreaming and astral travel with heightened intuition.

Obsidian – the multitude of colors in the crystal makes scrying more detailed and provides enhanced readings.

Opal - Traditionally an unlucky stone in divination, it helps the user induce visions from higher beings and increases intuition.

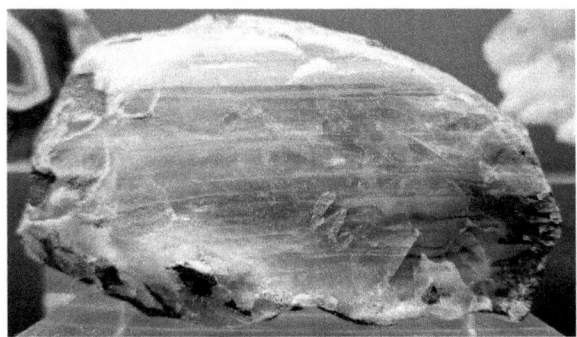

Opal increases intuition.
Eric Polk, CC BY-SA 4.0 <https://creativecommons.org/licenses/by-sa/4.0>, via Wikimedia Commons: https://commons.wikimedia.org/wiki/File:Opal_NHMLA.png

Quartz - Strengthens the crown chakra and boosts the third eye power meaning the user will experience stronger communication from the spirits and higher beings.

Sapphire - This gemstone brings different qualities depending on the color. Black is intuitive, while purple helps the user improve their dream recollections. Green sapphires increase psychic skills, and blue sapphires enhance the third eye chakra.

Sodalite - Increases psychic experiences and brings a deeper understanding of messages and visions.

Turquoise - This ancient stone has been used to bridge the veil between the physical and spiritual realms for thousands of years.

Turquoise can bridge the veil between the physical and spiritual realms.
Adrian Pingstone, Public domain, via Wikimedia Commons:
https://commons.wikimedia.org/wiki/File:Turquoise.pebble.700pix.jpg

Crystals and How to Use Them in Divination, Healing, and Spiritual Awareness

Divination with crystals can be performed in many guises, and you can experiment to find the method that suits your style. Seers have been using crystals to foretell the future for generations, and the process is called lithomancy.

Pendulum Dowsing with Crystals

Back in ancient Egypt, Hindu cultures, and Chinese history, there are many records of crystal divination using pendulums. The crystals were attached to a chain and held at height to achieve vibrations that indicated the message from beyond. Some seers would calibrate their pendulum by setting clear instructions on what each movement indicates. Two nudges to the left for yes and two to the right for no are the first calibration.

Today, many practitioners use pendulum wheels to get clearer answers and more detailed readings. They create a wheel of possibilities which is divided into 18 sections of 20 degrees to create 18 different specifics for your questions. These can include any details you feel are relevant to the questions you have about spirits and how they answer.

The crystals used in the pendulum are specific for the metaphysical answers you require, so using the relevant crystal increases the chance of gaining effective insight into your issues.

Which Crystal to Use in Your Pendulum:

- Rose crystals are the best for questions about love and relationships. Ask the spirits about your soulmates and true love and what your love life will look like in the future.
- Amethyst crystals help you find answers about your spiritual destiny and how your past life is affecting your karmic debt. Use the pendulum to answer questions that cause you anxiety and fear so you can feel calmer and more connected to your past and future existences.
- Sodalite helps you improve your communication and deal with negative energy. They increase your communication skills and connect you to the angels and your spiritual team. Use them in a pendulum to release any feelings of hatred and jealousy to regain your spiritual balance.

- Labradorite is the crystal of the Aurora Borealis and helps you answer questions about your destiny. It represents the power of healing and dream therapy and will help you feel more grounded in times of chaos and crisis.
- Red jasper pendulums increase your sense of confidence and courage. Use it to ask the spirits to help you feel more able to resolve conflicts without harm and to bring peace to your life.
- Black tourmaline helps you feel protected and safe from psychic attacks. If you feel you are psychically blocked, use a black tourmaline pendulum to open those blocked chakras and resume all forms of spiritual connections.

Crystals for Scrying

Scrying is divination gained from looking into clear surfaces and seeing visions. Perhaps the most traditional method is the crystal ball which has already been mentioned. Still, modern practitioners know that many different crystals will serve the purpose without buying a ball. The crystals absorb and store energy from the universe and help you tune into your higher self and the spirit world to gain insight and knowledge.

Black obsidian is a natural choice for scrying. With its deep black color, it is an effective way to see images. Try scrying in the light of a new moon to get results and stare into the crystal at eye level while you meditate upon what you want the crystal to show you. The results should include clear images of which spirits and subconscious beliefs are right for you.

Quartz crystal is a clear option for scrying and gives you clarity of vision on its unflawed surface. Try scrying in low light, by candle perhaps, and invite the spirits to show you their answers and suggestions.

Polar jade crystals are a popular choice for divination because of the depth of clarity they provide. It has been referred to as "The Stone of Power" by healers and seekers for generations, and it is effective in protection and connection to your higher self. It has powerful healing qualities and is used to process insights and enhance concentration.

Smoky quartz is perfect for beginners as it is a calming and grounding crystal that absorbs negative energy. It will keep you safe and protected during your divination and help you connect to the spirits effectively.

Crystals for Clairvoyance

Iolite

Also known as the Viking's compass, iolite was a key part of the Vikings' discovery of the New World as it reduced glare and polarized sunlight so the Viking sailors could navigate more effectively. The element of air rules iolite, increasing its ability to unlock dormant skills and abilities, including clairvoyance. If you lie on the floor and place an iolite crystal on your forehead between the brows, it helps you to boost your concentration and improve your memory.

Iolite can also clear your mind of mental chatter and increase your capacity for learning while it also helps boost your energy levels. Use an elixir made from iolite crystals and water to fill yourself with solar energy and positivity.

Kyanite

These crystals help you improve your clairvoyance skills and balance all the chakras in the body. It will flush out toxins from them and help you reclaim your intuition and gain hereditary magic from your ancestors. Wear it on your body to increase spiritual communication throughout your regular life.

Labradorite

Once again, the versatile crystal of labradorite helps you achieve clairvoyance. It is especially effective in stimulating your brain and teaching it how to recognize signs from the spirits. It activates the throat and third eye chakras, which make clairvoyance more achievable.

Amazonite for Ghostly Divinations

If your interest is piqued by communicating with ghosts, then consider using Amazonite crystals, which open up other realms and protect you from evil. The main difference between ghosts and spirits is that ghosts are always the souls of deceased people, while spirits could have lived on Earth but not necessarily in human form. Ghosts will appear to you in human form and can often present as their human form, and they feel and act differently to spirits.

Ghosts are often tied to their location due to the tragic circumstances of their passing, and some won't even realize they have passed. They may have tragic backgrounds and vibrate with chaotic energy, but very few of them wish you any harm. They may be confused and wish to complete unfinished business before they leave for the other realm, so if you do contact them, be prepared for a sad story or even anger. This is a specialized form of divination that beginners should not undertake. Once you have become accomplished with spiritual communications, then you could try divination with ghosts and use Amazonite for your rituals.

Sodalite for Tarot Readings

If you do struggle to interpret the sign you are getting from your tarot cards, try putting a sodalite crystal by your table. It will help you connect to your inner wisdom and find meaning in the cards. Sodalite also reminds you to look deeper at your reasons for asking the questions and tap into your unused intuition.

Serpentine for Angelic and Otherworldly Connections

Serpentine is thought to be powered by the energy of the Greek Gorgon Medusa, the powerful guardian who could turn men to stone with just one glance. It is a powerful way to connect to other realms and find guidance from the angels and spirits that reside far beyond Earth. It will help you find your way if you are lost in your crafting, feeling uninspired, and at a loss to know what to do next.

Lapis Lazuli for Finding Your Tether

Sometimes magic and witchcraft can get overwhelming, and you feel like your spirit work and spellcasting have become stale and are going nowhere. Trust in lapis lazuli to help you find your roots and to create a tether in the spirit world. Sometimes there is so much activity it can be hard to identify your lead guardian, so ask lapis lazuli to help you with your search.

Divination may seem like a new age activity and is a fun way to collect shiny crystals, tarot cards, and runes, but the practice has its roots deeply entrenched in ancient cultures. Buddhism, pagan, Judaism, and Christianity all have records of wise men or seers using divination to look into the future. Today, it is known that a lot of reading is powered by the subconscious, powered by the energy of the universe or the spirit world. You don't have to be religious or be affiliated with a certain belief to practice divination. You just have to believe.

Keep yourself safe with the normal rules of witchcraft and always be respectful of the practice. The spirits are always ready to communicate with us providing we show them that we are involved for the right reasons. If you use divination for fun and trivial matters, tell them and ask if they will indulge you. The questions you ask don't always have to be life-changing; they just have to be honest and come from a place of love.

Chapter 8: Lunar Magic

Different phases of the sun and moon.
https://unsplash.com/photos/83SUHaReev4

People take the moon and sun for granted. They know that both celestial bodies will be there every day, and the sun will bring warmth and light while the moon lights the night sky. It is impossible to imagine the world functioning without either, and that's because it wouldn't be able to.

Because of its magical properties, the moon is especially important and significantly affects how the Earth works and how humans feel emotionally. The power of lunar energy rules the tides and seas, and there is a reason why the word lunatic is used to describe a madman. Long ago, it was believed that humans behaved differently in the phases of the moon's cycle, and the same principles apply to magic. Every phase has the power to enhance your magic, providing you know how to use them.

Lunar magic is an archetype of magic, and the moon's powers have influenced mankind since time began. The moon has an incredible pull on mankind, and its cycles are intrinsic to magical powers. Most laypersons know the power of the full moon and what it brings to magic, but they are less aware of the properties of the other cycles. Witchcraft and magic will still work even if you aren't aware of which cycle the moon is in, but it is more likely to have more impressive results if you work with the moon and make sure the elements are all aligned for success. Just as in your regular life, the more resources you have available, the better the job gets done. It's worth delving into the different phases in-depth, but you may like to have a magical cheat sheet to start with. These simple breakdowns help remind you when to cast your spells and why. You can make them into reminders to keep by your altar or your magic tool store to use during your crafting.

The waxing moon is the time to:
- Draw money
- Attraction spells
- Progression and increasing spells
- Finding hidden talents
- Developing and pursuing new goals and skills

The full moon is the time to:
- Charge your crystals
- Work within a coven
- Work major spells
- Cast healing magic
- Raise power levels
- Wishing magic

The waning moon is the time to:
- Work on personal goals like weight loss
- Elimination spells
- Banishing magic
- Cleansing energies
- Moving on

The dark moon is the time for:
- Divination spells
- Consulting the oracle
- Starting new projects
- New beginnings
- Setting strong intentions

Magic for the Waxing Moon

This is the cycle of abundance, and like riding a wave inland, it makes things move more quickly and with more intention. This is the time to set spells for personal success and growth.

The spells below will give you a clear idea of how this cycle works, so go ahead and cast those spells for beauty and abundance. You deserve it.

Create a Plan for Personal Growth

On the first day of the waxing moon, start with a blank piece of paper and a pen. Write down what you plan to achieve and what outcomes would be best for you. Consider your relationship, your career, or your finances. What could improve these areas of your life? Now you have a blueprint for your success, and you can cast spells to perform rituals to make sure they happen. Start with a clear plan and prepare to celebrate your success when the full moon appears.

A Money Drawing Spell

What do your finances look like? Are you in debt, or would you simply like a bit more cash coming in? Use the waxing moon cycle to draw money into your life and create moneymaking opportunities.

Set out a place for you to sit in the moonlight on the first night of the waxing moon. Bring a green candle and a representative of money like a dollar bill or your wallet. Sit in meditation beneath the moonlight and say the following spell:

"Lunar power, come to me, bring me luck and wealth, fill my wallet and my life with abundance and love, and make it so."

Let the candle burn down naturally and bury the wax in the ground. When you have completed the spell, you will start to notice new ways to earn money. Maybe someone will ask you to pet sit for them, or a new position becomes available at work. Whatever you are given, be sure to take them even if they are things you haven't considered in the past.

Cast a Love and Attraction Spell
The Honey Jar Spell

This is part of most witches' spells 101, and it is a powerful and effective spell to boost relationships. This could be used for romantic purposes or to bring added strength to friendships. The honey spell is about creating intimacy and deeper connections, so casting it during the waxing moon phase will work even more effectively.

What You Need:
- Paper and pen
- A jar filled with honey
- A red candle for passionate love, a white candle for general purposes, or a pink candle for friendship

How to Cast the Spell
1. Write the name of the other person on the piece of paper.
2. Turn the paper around for 90 degrees and then write your name on the paper three times until it completely covers the other name on the paper.
3. Close your eyes and visualize what you see for the two of you in the future before you write that intention around the two names.
4. Now add the paper to the honey-filled jar – covering the paper completely.
5. Make sure you get some of the honey on your fingers before saying:

"Just like this honey is sweet, that's how our relationship will be."

6. Slowly lick the honey from your fingers while you repeat the words of intent.
7. Seal the jar with a lid.
8. Place the appropriate candle on the top of the jar and light it.
9. Let the candle burn naturally, and let the wax seal the jar.
10. Store the jar away until the next waxing moon cycle.
11. Repeat the spell until you have achieved your desires.

Cast spells for joy, happiness, healing, social growth, pregnancy, and other attraction sources in the waxing moon, and your life will soon start to feel the benefit.

Magic for the Full Moon

There are three days when the power of the full moon is at its height. The day before and the day after the full moon are just as powerful as the actual day, and this is when you should perform your most impressive magic. In this part of the chapter, you will find simple ways to use the power of the full moon.

Charge Your Crystals

Create a space outside where you can see the full moon clearly. Ensure the space is clean and large enough for all your crystals to be without touching each other. Place a cloth on the space and carefully arrange your crystals so they benefit from the moonlight. Leave your crystals in the moonbeams for two hours and then take them back inside. They will be pure and clean and free from negative energy.

Release Things Holding You Back

This ritual helps you use the power of the archangels to help you move on. Invoke the archangel Haniel to aid you in this ritual before you perform it. Take a piece of paper and write down everything holding you back. Is it your job, or do you have bad habits? Are there things about your partner you wish were different, or do you need to detox your life?

When you have your list invoke the power of Haniel and thank him for his presence, light the paper on fire and close your eyes as you imagine your issues burning away into the atmosphere. When you open your eyes, watch the smoke leave and imagine it carrying your negativity with it. Close your eyes once more and ask Haniel if he has a message for you. Whatever flashes before you will give you the answer you need.

Full Moon Wish Spell
What You Need:
- A clear jar with a lid
- Rainwater that has been charged in the moonlight
- A silver coin
- A bell
- A silver candle

Choose a space where you can work in the moonlight and in full view of the moon. Hold the coin and focus on your desires, wishes, and what you want from life. Light the silver candle.

When you feel ready, drop the coin into the jar. Pour the water into the jar while you let it charge in the moonlight. When the water is smooth, and the reflection of the moon is clearly seen on the surface, say these words:

"*This is my wish, and I ask that you grant it.*"

Ring the bell and then state your wish loudly and with intent. Repeat the process three times before placing the lid on the jar. Take the candle and drip some wax on the top of the lid before you thank the spirits for their help and go indoors with all your materials.

Keep the coin in the jar until you feel your wish has been granted or until the next full moon, when you can repeat the spell to reinforce your wishes.

Magic for the Waning Moon

Release and let go in this cleansing period of the moon. How does negativity affect you, and how can you become more positive? Magic and rituals performed in the waning moon period are especially effective when clearing out your spiritual and physical lives.

Cleansing Your Environment

Where do you feel the most protected and safe from negativity? Your home should be a haven, and your sacred space should all be clear from negativity, but just like regular cleaning, there are many different ways to cleanse your spaces. Some methods work better for some, while others are suitable for certain spaces where there are restrictive elements.

When to Cleanse Your Spaces

The rule of thumb is to cleanse whenever somewhere feels "off" or you don't feel as comfortable and safe as normal. However, sometimes you need to cleanse after certain events or before you perform certain rituals. Here are some of the most common:

- Your home after there have been disputes or arguments
- Your bed and bedroom after you have had nightmares or dreams that have left you anxious and stressed
- Your altar or sacred space after a spell has gone wrong or was ineffective
- There won't always be negative energy in your altar or sacred space after you have connected with spirits or ancestors. Still, it

is important to clear residual energy between communications.
- Your tools and divination aids between readings and spells
- The bath or bathroom before you have a ritual bath
- Work areas after negative experiences and unsuccessful projects

Different Kinds of Cleansing Routines

Water Cleansing

The most available and adaptable way to cleanse is with pure water. Moon water is the most effective way to bring lunar energy to your space, but pure water also works. Fill a clear jug or bowl with water and ask the spirits to bless the liquid. Walk around your space clockwise, flicking the water around the perimeter. This method is effective for routine cleansing and is very budget-friendly.

Salt Clearing

This method is especially effective for hard surfaces and floors. Replace the water with sea salt and sprinkle it around the perimeter of your area. Leave it for an hour before you sweep it up and throw it away. Remember to remove the residue salt from the home and dispose of it away from your immediate environment. Be careful when cleansing a carpeted area, as the salt can sometimes react with the dye in carpets.

Musical Clearing

This method is a joyful way to get rid of dodgy vibes. You know the feeling when you aren't sure why, but the hairs on the back of your neck are standing up, and you just feel icky. Creepy vibes and nervous energy aren't ideal, so use this method for an injection of positivity and joy. Crank up your radio or get out an old-school record player and bust out music that speaks to you. Upbeat hip-hop or classic rock tunes work especially well and dispel that negativity and anxious energy. Choose music to suit your situation.

Smoke Cleansing

This traditional method uses herbs and smudge sticks to cleanse spaces. Of course, some spaces won't be suitable, and some people have issues with smoke. If the space is suitable, then use sage bundles and smudge sticks to fill the area with cleansing smoke to clear negativity and bad vibes.

Essential Oils Cleanse

This is a method used to clear spaces that have been subject to major disruptions. It is a heavy-duty cleanse that ensures the space is harmonized and negativity-free. Choose the oils you love or are suitable for the situation and anoint all four corners of the space with them. Use a diffuser to cover the rest of the area while you call on the spirits for their blessing.

Breath Cleansing

What if the space you need cleansing is within yourself, and you feel blocked? Clear your mind and aura with this simple routine and lift your spirits and mood. Clean your teeth and mouth thoroughly before you sit in a quiet place where you won't be disturbed. Breathe in for a count of 5 and breathe out for a count of 6. Visualize a calm and soothing place where you feel safe and imagine yourself in it. Feel a blanket of calm surround you as you repeat the breathing g exercise until you feel calm and settled.

Magic for the Dark Moon

When the moon has all but left the sky, this is the perfect time to honor your ancestors and explore your unconscious mind. Take a deep delve into your subconscious and do some serious soul-searching. Take a hot ritual bath with your favorite herbs and oils to release tensions and built-up trauma.

Use these methods to banish drama and get your life back on track:

Banishing Candle Method
What You Need:
- Two whole cloves of garlic
- Four whole peppercorns
- ¼ liter of olive oil
- Black candle
- Carving tool

Soak the garlic and peppercorns in olive oil for two days before the dark moon. Carve the word "drama" into the candle when it is time to perform the ritual. If you have more specific issues, use different words to represent what is troubling you. Anoint the candle with the oil using a downward motion. Let the oil run off until the candle is fully ready for use. Place it in a candle holder and light it beneath the dark moon at night. Say a few words to the spirits, let the candle completely burn away, and then bury the remnants.

Bury the Drama Method

Do you have long-standing issues that have followed you through history? Are you fed up with tiring issues that keep reappearing? Take a piece of paper and list the conflicts and issues troubling you. Be detailed and clear about the problem, and ensure you are happy with the list.

On the night of the dark moon, take a small hand shovel, some blessed dirt, and the paper containing your issues. Go somewhere far from your home and bury the paper deep in the ground. Place the blessed dirt on top of the site and leave. Walk away and don't look back.

Spell to Break a Bad Habit

The burying process is effective at the dark moon and can be used to eliminate a bad habit.

What You Need:
- Small wooden box
- Pen and paper
- Clove of garlic
- 2 pieces of rosemary
- Symbol of your bad habit (a cigarette lighter, for example)
- A handful of coins
- Spade

The first thing to remember is that habits are hard to quit, and you need to be sure it's what you want. Write all the reasons for quitting on paper and keep it somewhere you can see it whenever you want to remind yourself why you are on this path.

During the full moon, charge your wooden box in the moonlight before you place it in your sacred space for two weeks. Every time you think about your bad habit during those two weeks, place a coin in the box. At first, this will happen a lot, but it should become less regular as the weeks pass.

Add garlic and rosemary to the box on the first night of the dark moon. Place the symbol inside as well and close the lid. Take the time to mourn the loss of something that has been with you for a long time before you shut the lid completely, and maybe nail it down or glue it shut.

Bury the box somewhere you love. A place with running water is best, as the motion of the water will help to take away the intent. Walk away and don't look back.

Moon Magic Overview

Whatever the cycle or season, it is important to chart how you work with lunar energy. Take one night per quarter to sit beneath the moon and consider how you feel. Are you tired or energized by the energy? Do you feel any more connected at certain times, or is the moon an effective way to practice mindfulness for you? If you are a Wiccan practitioner, you will already know the power of the esbat, which is a pagan time of power.

Transition to a moon-centric life, benefit from its celestial power, and improve your crafting. Lunar witchcraft is overwhelming because it's so powerful, so start small and build up your expertise to enhance your regular life and crafting life.

Chapter 9: Spirit Guides

Ingesting psychoactive plants is believed to connect you to the plant elements of nature.
https://unsplash.com/photos/SzwyWBHwLMk

Who is on your team? In your regular life, it could be your partner, your best friend, your family, someone at work who is always there for you, or someone from the gym who helps you work out. Your social circle is your team, filled with people you can trust, love, and have your back. But what about your spiritual team? Who is part of the team that guides you through your magical life, and how are they relevant in your regular life? This chapter is all about the spirit guides and how they are part of your life, even if you don't realize they are there.

In Western spiritualism beliefs, multiple types of guides are assigned to your team, and it is their spiritual purpose to act as a guide or protector to you. They may have been on your team in previous lives or may be new to this incarnation. Your team, just like your regular social circle, changes and adapts to your needs. Some guides will be with you from your first incarnation and will be there until you ascend, while others will pop in and out of your life when you need them.

Another fascinating fact about your spiritual team is that they may or may not have spent time on Earth as humans. Some may be from astral planes and extraterrestrial systems, while others may live in light planes. Some may be angels and archangels who are dedicated to guiding you no matter which religion you follow. It is a common misconception that angels and archangels only help Christians. In spiritual terms, they serve mankind and have no interest in your religious beliefs.

Your main spirit guide is always there for you and was assigned to your life - long before this earthly existence. They know every fiber of your being and will help you whenever needed. Spirit guides are benevolent and loving, and they never judge you or your actions but may intervene if they feel you are on the wrong path. They are dedicated to guiding you and helping you achieve a specific and dedicated purpose in your current lifetime. You have complete autonomy when making decisions; your spirit team will always help you get what you desire.

Are There Any Spirits to Avoid?

Of course, not all spirits are equal. The main thing to remember is that the energy you send into the world will mirror the energy of the spirits you attract. In regular life, you wouldn't just ask a stranger for advice; you need to know that the person is on the same moral plane as you are to get important information. Just like the advice you gave about connecting to deities, the spirits are the same. There are low-level vibrational beings who aren't matched to your frequency and should be avoided. They aren't necessarily malignant or harmful but can affect you if you connect to them.

You can just say goodbye and disconnect if you feel connected to a spirit that doesn't match your frequency. Don't be disrespectful; thank them as you would in regular communications and say a respectful goodbye. You need to use your intuition and common sense to determine who and what you connect to, so apply this to your spirit team and gather the most positive and effective spirits you can.

Meet the Team

1. Life Guides or Guardian Angels

These spirits are your go-to energies who never leave your side. They operate on a higher energy level than humans and are always ready to impart their knowledge and wisdom. You may already know who they are from your former lives. They may have a name and a recognizable form in your mind. They are the "office managers" of your team, and they know how to deal with chaos and will keep an eye on the rest of your team. They bring peace and love to your existence and are happy to be there. Remember to connect to your guardian angels by asking them about their background as a spirit. These conversations deepen your connection and help you understand their ethos.

2. Warriors and Protectors

These are your personal bodyguards who are dedicated to keeping you safe, both physically and spiritually. Have you ever had a gut feeling about something that made you rethink your actions or plans? That could be your warrior guide telling you that something isn't quite right.

Warrior spirits are incredibly enlightened and will work with you to filter out any adverse advice and guidance that isn't dedicated to helping you achieve your highest purpose. They will often appear to you as literal warriors, soldiers, or other defensive forms. If you happen to see a sumo wrestler or a Viking warrior in your dreams or visions, say hello to your warrior spirit guide.

3. Gatekeeper Guides

These are another protective form of the spirit. They act as your doorman and check everything that passes into your life. Gatekeepers are incredibly important, and they have access to your Akashic record. This is the spiritual blueprint of your life and contains information about your past, present and future lives. They only allow energy sources that are dedicated to bringing you high-level and loving forms of energy.

4. Teacher Guides

As the name indicates, these spirits are there to teach you lessons. They are incredibly wise and practical, and they will visit you when you are straying from the path you are on. They aren't judging you; they simply need to point out your choices and give you alternative ways to go. Some people fear their teacher guides but, in reality, they are some of the more effective guides you have. They appear to you when you need to assess your current situation and maybe change course.

5. Animal or Totem Guides

Modern witchcraft and pagans have "rediscovered" the power of the animal spirit. Some ancient cultures like the Chinese and American Indians have known for generations just how important spirit animals are, and you can benefit from your own connection to the animal world. Your spirit animals reflect your inner yearnings and personality. You will connect on many levels, and they will mirror your work ethic, your passions, and how you instinctively operate. Some people believe they can choose their spirit animal, but that isn't true. You may imagine you have connections with "cool "animals like dolphins or eagles, but your spirit animal chooses you. It could be a spider or a cat, a snake, or a dog. You need to meditate and reflect so your animal appears to you in your dreams or visions.

6. Ancestors

Many ancient cultures have rituals and ceremonies to celebrate the dead and their ancestors. They offer food and drink to the spirits of those who have passed over and welcome them back to earth. In modern witchcraft, you can also tap into the hidden energies of your relatives. They bring blood connections that are historical and personal. Meeting your ancestors and your family's spirits will help you feel part of your lineage and can be beautiful and life-changing. Some ancestral spirits will be members of your family you have known, while some of them will be long-dead relatives who lived way before your lifetime.

7. Trans-species

Modern life is very aware of trans and what it means in sexuality. Still, there are also trans spirits that embody the connection between mankind and the animal world. Consider ancient spirit guides and the forms they took to give you inspiration about what to expect. The Indian god Ganesha was a human form with an elephant's head. In contrast, Anubis, the Egyptian god, had the head of a jackal. Echidna in Greek mythology was half woman and half snake, while Ra, the Egyptian god, was a human man with a falcon's head.

Groups of Spirits that Fall into this Category

- **The Centaur** – From Greek mythology, this half-man/half-horse creature has gained more attention since the Harry Potter books and films. It originates from the times of the Minoan civilization. It is believed they were so impressed by other cultures who rode horses that they created the myth of the centaur.
- **The Harpy** – In both Greek and Roman tales, the harpy is a bird with a woman's head who was described as a "human vulture." They represent destructive winds and signify the clearance of negative energy.
- **The Gorgon** – The three sisters from Greek mythology who were the most terrifying therianthrope ever were the gorgons, who were women in every way except for their terrifying hair made of writhing and hissing serpents. Simply looking at them would render humans into half-man/half-horse stone, and it is believed they are the original representation of the fear of snakes. Some gorgons are depicted with scales and claws, but the most recognizable are the ones with reptilian hair.
- **The Mermaid** – The original legend came from Assyria and told of a beautiful maiden with the tail of a fish who had transformed herself into mermaid form in shame after she accidentally killed her human lover. These creatures often appear to help seamen and sailors and could be part of your spiritual team.

Other trans spirits include faeries, sphinxes, and fauns, and they can be playful and entertaining creatures who visit you when you need to experience truly magical energy.

8. Ascension and Soul Guides

Some of your guides will be directly related to your soul's age and the level of your ascension. If you are an old soul, you will be given a guide appropriate to your level. If you are new to the process, the same principle applies. Just as in regular life, you are given the information you need depending on your experience and soul age.

9. Plants

In shamanic practices, ingesting plants that have psychoactive elements is believed to connect you to the plant energies of nature. Shamans believe that plants are a major source of vibrant and living energy, and they hold rituals and ceremonies to celebrate this fact. Certain species of cacti and acacia can create the same experience, but they can be dangerous. Suppose you want to summon the spirits of the plant world. In that case, it is safer to concentrate on the symbolic plant world rather than the experiential experiences.

10. Ascended Master

These are the "celebrities" of the spirit world. They have lived as humans, and they have mastered the spiritual aspects of life. Their experience of spiritual transcending and their ability to rise above the cycle of reincarnation makes them the ultimate teachers - providing you with an insight into the divine. They are available to everyone who calls on them as long as their intentions are true and come from the right place. They aren't strictly part of your team but are always on the sidelines, ready to be called if needed. They have paid their karmic debt and mastered ascension.

Common Ascended Masters

- **Jesus** - The ultimate ascended master who gave his life to save mankind. He brings the energy of unconditional love and joy. He teaches and displays the ultimate form of forgiveness as he forgave those that crucified him.
- **The Archangels** - It seems dismissive to link all the Archangels in one group, but they are the epitome of what ascended masters look like. Each of the angels brings different qualities, and they can work together as a team within their ranks to help you. Study them and discover what they bring to your life before you call on these heavenly beings to become part of your team. Remember, the angels don't care if you are religious or not. They have bigger things to think about, and they have the ear of God.
- **Amoghasiddhi** - In Buddhism, this deity is the destroyer of envy and the bringer of accomplishment. He will help you overcome jealousy and get past your obstacles when needed.

- **Krishna** – The eighth incarnation of the Hindu god Vishnu Krishna is wise and compassionate, bringing healing and love to your life.
- **Milarepa** – The famous Tibetan yogi who founded the school of Tibetan Buddhism and is a spiritual embodiment of joy. He is famous for his poetry and songs and will inspire you to be more creative and loving.
- **Mother Teresa** – The Albanian Catholic nun who taught the world the meaning of true compassion and was a leading light in the Church. Call on her for kindness and love when you feel like you need more humanity in your life.

How to Connect to Your Spirit Guides

You can use the same methods as described in the chapter about gods and goddesses, and you will get a response. The methods below are more dedicated to certain groups and spirits and intensify your intent which is the base of all good magic.

Ancestors

Your ancestors are waiting for you in the spirit world, and there are many ways to connect to them. Start a family tree and research your ancestors. So many online resources are available that it is easy to find where you came from. Another way to connect to your more recent ancestors is to use objects that once belonged to them. Maybe you have a piece of jewelry or a favorite item of clothing that you associate with your relatives. Hold it close and let your mind clear of anything except your memories. Ask them to visit you, share their life experiences, and guide you for the future.

Your ancestors will respond and bring the unmistakable feeling of family to your life. You will feel uplifted and joyful. Increase this connection by wearing your items or displaying them in your home. There doesn't have to be a shrine to your relatives, just a place where you can remember them and be thankful for their influence.

The Archangels or Other Ascended Masters

Connecting to the highest members of the spiritual realm is daunting for beginners, but that doesn't mean you shouldn't try. The spirits have a hierarchy, but they are also benevolent beings dedicated to helping humankind live better lives. They won't ever push themselves forward or interfere if you don't ask first. They respect free will and your personal choices and will never visit unless summoned.

Research your spirits and get to know them just like you did with the gods and goddesses. What did they achieve on Earth? What were they known for, and why are you drawn to them? Your instinct will tell you whom to communicate with and why.

Simple Steps to Better Communication

Step 1 – Get into the Habit of Asking

When you encounter smaller problems during your regular life, try calling on spirits or the universe for help. The more you ask, the more you will receive, and the process will become more natural. Think of them as a helpline that is always there and ready to take your call.

Step 2 – Make a List of What You Need

Vague doesn't work with spirit guides. The clearer your requests are (and the more details you provide), the more effective your spirit guides are. Take the time to list the top issues in your life and what effect they are having on your life. Be concise yet clear, and write them down with intent and belief that this is the first step in dealing with your issues.

Step 3 – Listen and See the Signs

Once you have put your requests out there, the onus is on you to recognize the signs you are sent.

Signs Your Spirits Are Communicating with You

- **You feel peaceful and calm.** If you feel as if someone is looking over your shoulder and keeping you safe, it helps you feel comforted. Fear and doubt leave you, and you feel optimistic and joyful.

- **You see signs that mean something to you.** The spirits are playful and like to mix it up a bit when it comes to communicating. They will send signs and symbols that are personal to your life and repeat them until you have dealt with your issues. Watch out for repeated symbols that have special meanings to you.

- **You get sudden ideas and insights** – If you get a "lightbulb moment" after you have asked for help from the spirit world, it could be a communication from them. They have the power to send you mental images or ideas to guide you in the right direction.
- **You receive information from unexpected sources.** If you suddenly see an opportunity to do something that wasn't there before, it could indicate the presence of spiritual aid. They will give you chances to take specific actions that might not make sense but will help you if you are brave enough to take them. Trust your instincts and the fact that this information will help you.
- **Physical sensations.** Some people say they feel physical sensations when they connect to the spirits. Warm-tingling feelings and pressure in certain areas could indicate they are with you.
- **Physical signs.** Spirits are great at sending you signs from nature that show they are around. Feathers are a popular choice and often appear to show you aren't alone. Some say birds appear in their garden when they lose a loved one or another random animal suddenly appears. Watch out for these signs and say thank you when you see them.

Ground Yourself after Connecting to the Spirit World

Connecting to the spirits is a physical and mental process. Eventually, you will have to return to your physical form on Earth. The energy shift you experience isn't practical for regular life, so you need to ground yourself and become involved in the wholly human existence your body is used to. Here are some simple methods to return to the planet and regain your equilibrium:

- Stamp your feet and feel the energy drain into the ground below your feet.
- Sit on a stone or rock and let the energy be absorbed by its natural material.
- Take care of yourself with a drink or snack to show you are back in charge of looking after yourself.

- Create a barrier by imagining a white light surrounding you. Once you are in your bubble, you will return to your natural state.

Remember that all the suggestions in this chapter won't work for everyone, but they do give you a blueprint for your communications. The spirits are there for you and will help you become part of the spiritual universe.

Chapter 10: Ritual Magic

Ritual magic may sound like something that is only available for advanced witches and practitioners. It sounds like the epic form of magic that needs to be studied and practiced for effective results. It does involve art and science, and it helps you to transform and change your life so that you become empowered and can create the life you choose. It is a magic practice that allows you to harness the abilities of your racial memory and tap into the powers and memories of humanity through time.

When the ancient Egyptians practiced ritual magic, their knowledge and practices became part of that collective story of magic. When Babylonians or Hindu cultures created new ways to communicate with the spirits and demons of their beliefs, that knowledge was also added to the primordial magic soup waiting for you to dine upon.

Your unconscious mind will be reminded of these racial memories and knowledge without you realizing it, and it will allow you to recognize symbols and signs from history. The collective realms of magic, higher thoughts, dreams, and creation are there for you and have been around since the dawn of creation. Across the world, different cultures have been practicing ritual magic, and they didn't limit their beliefs to science. Only in the last few generations have humans regressed into the childish belief that if they can't recognize something with their physical senses, then it isn't and can't be true. Humans have become a race of people who think if they can't measure it, then it doesn't exist.

Ritual Magic in Today's Terms

Ritual magic is one of the most powerful forms of magic, and it can give you direct access to higher energies from countless realms that will bring real changes to your life. It is performed with all parts of yourself and immerses your mind, soul, body, and deepest intentions in the ritual so the ceremony and the magic become like another extension of yourself. The practice, also known as ceremonial magic, gained popularity in the late 19th and early 20th centuries.

An influx of pagan beliefs and occult practices meant that ceremonies and rituals became more popular, and the occultist Alastair Crowley was one of the most effective advocates. The ceremonies and rituals were steeped in secrecy to ensure the practitioners were able to perform their ceremonies without recrimination. Today, the practice is more open and involves deepening your focus and building your practice, so the magic is more powerful. It isn't a practice for casual magic. This will change your life and how you engage with your subconscious mind. It is a step further on your journey and will help you embrace a life of transformation and progression.

Ritual Magic Techniques

Previous chapters have covered some more popular techniques like divination, invoking, and evoking spirits and deities. Other techniques happen in ceremonial magic, like the Eucharist magic ritual that has evolved from Christianity and involves the digestion of regular foods that have been made divine. This is called Holy Communion, an important part of the Christian belief.

Consecration is another form of ceremonial magic involving dedicating a space or person as a sacred sphere used for a magical purpose and service.

Banishing is the most used form of ritual magic and can be used to remove non-physical influences from your life. One of the more effective rituals is the Lesser Banishing Ritual of the Pentagram, described below.

The Lesser Banishing Ritual of the Pentagram

This ritual magic will give a greater insight into how the process works and the power of your intent. It can be adapted to your needs and requirements and the deities and spirits with whom you work.

Step 1. Stand in the middle of a sacred space and face east. Imagine you are a giant sculpture looking down on the planet as a tiny sphere in your eye line. You are the center of the universe, and everything revolves around you. Look up and see the bright white light that emanates from above you and pull it down to your forehead.

Step 2. Hold the beam of light as if it was a dagger, and repeat the word ATAH as you feel the vibrations.

Step 3. Move your right hand down your body, passing over your throat, chest, and groin area as you feel the white light running right through you. There is now a beam of white energy and light running from the top of the universe to the Earth, and it passes right through your body. Say the word MALKUTH as you feel the connection form.

Step 4. Raise your hand to your right shoulder and imagine the white light is drawn to that point. Now visualize the light emanating from your shoulder and into the universe. Say the word VEGEBOORA as the light passes through you.

Step 5. Repeat the process with your left shoulder, replacing the word with VEGEDOOLA.

Step 6. Now center yourself by raising your arms to your chest as if you were praying and clasp them together. Say the words LAYOLAM AMEN. You are now the central part of a cross with light emanating from you to the very edges of the universe. You are now the ruler of your universe and the creator of your destiny.

Step 7. Now face the east and trace a large five-sided pentagram with your finger. Imagine that lines are formed by flaming, bright-blue lights, and the pentacle glows with the power of a thousand lamps. Bring your hands back to the side of your head and point your fingers forward. As you do so, thrust your left foot before you and say the word YODAYVAVHEH. This is the Hebrew signal of the enterer and shows the universe your intent to march forward and to capture the energy of your life.

Feel the divine energy running through you and being absorbed by the pentagram. Take your left foot and replace it in its former position so you are standing straight. Now raise your left hand and put your index finger to your mouth to signal silence. Your right arm should remain extended and pointing to the pentagram.

Step 8. Start to walk backward to the southern part of your area with your finger still retaining a connection to the blue pentagram. Create a white line of blazing energy between yourself and the symbol. As you reach the southernmost point, you will have created a circle of energy between the symbol and yourself.

Trace another pentagram in the air and say the word ADONAY as you see the flames burst into life. Repeat this process in the west as you vibrate the word EEHAYYAY. Do the same in the north, saying AGALA, and then walk to the east to complete the circle.

Step 9. Look at the circle you have created. Four magnificent pentagrams at the cardinal points of your space, all joined by a circle of pure white energy.

Step 10. Step into the center of the area, recreate the magical cross of Kabbalistic energy and invoke the angel Gabriel by saying his name. Imagine he is standing behind you dressed in magnificent robes of orange and blue, and his favored element, water, is flowing onto your back.

Step 11. Now open your eyes and look to the right of yourself and say, "On my right, Michael," and visualize the archangel of fire standing beside you. His robes are red and green, and you can feel the heat of his favorite element, fire, heating your body.

Step 12. Extend your arms and invoke the archangel of air, RAPHAEL and visualize him standing in his robes of yellow and violet and feel the cooling energy of his element, air, on your face and body.

Step 13. Look over your left shoulder and invoke the archangel of earth, AURIEL, dressed in russet and green robes. Feel the solidity of his energy enter your body and make you feel grounded and safe.

Step 14. Take a minute to visualize what you have created. An amazing circle of energy with a blazing pentagram and the presence of archangels. Say,

"*Around me shines these pentagrams,*"

and now trace the shape of a hexagon in a brilliant orange fire on your breast. Say,

"*Within me shines the power of the six-pointed star.*"

as you finish the ritual.

Use this ritual to banish negativity and ask the archangels to change your life and imbue you with the strength of the universe. This circle is impenetrable and will protect you from all negative forces and influences.

How to Cast a Wiccan Ritual Magic Circle

This is a simple protection ritual that you can perform anywhere and can be modified to suit your needs and the time of year you are performing your magic. Use the wheel of the year to help you choose ritualistic items that celebrate the power of nature. If you are short on space, just use the four-candle part of the ritual for a temporary and effective ritual.

1. Choose a space and set the scene by playing music that inspires you as you work.
2. Cleanse the area with a ritual broom only used for magic, not regular housework, helping you set the scene.
3. Use candles to mark the cardinal points of the room. Red for the south, blue for the west, green for the north, and yellow for the east.
4. Move clockwise and light the candles while saying a prayer of thanks to your chosen spirits or deities.
5. Use markers to form a circle between the candles. Natural objects like branches or flowers work and increase the connection to nature.
6. Take a bowl of water and bless it with these words:
   "I consecrate this liquid to make it fit for a place in my sacred circle, and I ask that it is blessed by the Mother and Father Gods (or your chosen deities) and are capable of repelling evil."
7. Now take a bowl of salt and say these words:
   "I ask the Mother and Father to consecrate this salt and make it fit to dwell within the sacred circle."
8. Imagine the water and salt dispersing all the negative energy in the room and leaving behind a cleansed and sacred space. Walk around the circle and say the following words:
   "Here is my sacred boundary; let nothing but love enter,
   There will be no negativity in this space,
   It is sacred and free from evil,
   So let it be."
9. Sprinkle the salt around the circle and seal it against negative energy. Say your favored chants and ask your preferred spirits to join you.

Your circle is now cast. This is your ritual magic space, and it can be used to call on the universe to make your life more effective and successful.

Tips for Ritual Magic

There are many rituals you can perform within your sacred space, and you should choose ones that suit your needs. The main things to remember about ritual or ceremonial magic are:

1. Stay safe. Create a sacred space that is strong and pure and will keep out negative energies and spirits that may not be fully on your wavelength.
2. Use tools to help your magic intentions become more pronounced. See the list below for a quick start-up guide for magic tools.
3. Use astrology to strengthen your spells and rituals. We have already covered lunar magic, but you can also use your zodiac sign to help you work when it is more effective. The stars will help you find your most powerful times of the year and when to perform certain spells.
4. Use your divination tools like tarot and the runes as part of your ritual magic. They may show you alternative ways to craft your spells.
5. Consider the ethics and morality of your magic. Are you true to your basic principles? Never perform magic that goes against your morals and beliefs, even when it seems advantageous to do so. Your intentions should always be true and free from negative emotional influences.

Magic Tools and How to Use Them

- **The Athame** - A magic dagger that represents the element of air and the sharpness of the mind. Use it to cast your circles and direct energy in your spells and rituals.
- **A Cup** - A ritual cup should only be used for magic purposes. Never use it to drink a cup of coffee or other regular liquids. The cup represents the element of water and is used to share libations or offer them to the deities and spirits. It represents the breath of your unconscious and the emotional ties to magic.

- **A Wand** - Traditionally made from wood or metal, a wand is an extension of the user and represents the will of the person wielding it. Use it to direct energy and increase focus.
- **Lamp** - Some practitioners prefer to use a lamp for spells rather than candles or fire, as they are a hazard. A lamp represents the element of spirit and the godhood within us all. It is also used to bring the power of the Holy Guardian Angel to your work.
- **The Besom** - This is a broom usually made from natural materials that are bound by willow strands. You can buy them from shops, but the most effective besoms are handmade. Use your favorite wood and create a besom for sweeping and clearing your sacred space.
- **The Pentacle** - Not to be confused with the pentagram, which is the five-sided figure used in the Lesser Banishing Ritual of the Pentagram. A pentacle is a flat piece of wood, metal, clay, or wax that is decorated with magical symbols. Once again, you can buy highly decorative pentacles from magical stores and online resources, but the most effective are ones that you create yourself. The pentacle is used as a base for your other magical tools and brings extra meaning to your work.
- **Robes** - The clothes you wear can make a huge difference in your crafting. Just like in regular life, preparing for your rituals and spellcasting should be thorough and done with intent. If you are going to your regular work, you dress appropriately in clothing that is suitable and fit for purpose. The same principle works for magic. Dress in loose and comfortable robes but make the occasion special with certain colors or styles of the robe. Your clothing helps you to get into the perfect state of mind for your work and focuses your attention.

Bonus Chapter: The Herbal Glossary

Witchcraft is all about using natural products to create magical potions and spells, but knowing what each ingredient brings to the situation is important. This list gives you basic knowledge which you can add to and helps you create an herb glossary that will help you with any spells you try.

Allspice - Brings money, prosperity, and luck to your magic. Also helps digestion and can be used as a general anesthetic.

Basil - Success in business opportunities and money. Brings calm energy and peaceful vibes to your crafting. When added to your cooking, it can also cure flatulence.

Bay Leaves - Used in banishment spells and exorcisms, bring fidelity and love to spells for relationships and strengthens wish magic. Use for stronger energies in spells to create luck, love, and passion.

Cayenne - Speeds up spells and brings extra strength to magic. Overcomes grief and loss and helps to aid separation.

Cloves - Stops gossip and aids protection.

Dill Weed - Luck, money, prosperity, and protection.

Fennel - Increased mental strength, helps weight-loss spells and brings fortitude and strength.

Garlic - Makes other ingredients more effective, protects against psychic vampires, and repels evil.

Ginger - Healing, soothing energy and creates new opportunities, and strengthens resolve.

Marjoram - Increased energy in ancestral magic, animal connections, and helps lucid dreaming, and is soothing.

Mandrake - Legendary magical herb for love magic, passion, relationship issues, protection, and curses

Marjoram - Protection. Helps marriages find common ground, calms the mind, eases grief, and aids in coming to terms with death.

Marshmallow Root - Love charms and amulets, increases psychic powers, protection, attracting positive spirits.

Meadowsweet - The sacred flower of spring, helps any new ventures and helps emotional rebirth.

Mistletoe - Good luck, love, and money spells, attracting potential life partners.

Mugwort - Mirror and water scrying, divination, psychic ability, astral travel, improves the chance of lucid dreaming, Lunar magic.

Mullein - Protection, illumination, clear mental health, bravery and courage, hedge-crossing, Crone magic.

Nettle - Courage, making spells more sacred, protection, healing, warding off evil.

Nutmeg - Brings luck, prosperity, and financial success.

Onion Flowers - Burn to banish bad habits and negative influences. Use raw onions to protect your home and keep evil spirits away.

Orange Peel - Raises vibrations and centering solar herb of joy, blessings, love, and good luck.

Orris Root - Love amulets and charms, increases powers of persuasion, increases popularity, charisma, and success.

Patchouli - Love and sex magic, attraction, fertility, rites of passage, and leaving adolescence behind.

Pennyroyal - Peace, increases mental and physical strength, patience, removing anger, warding.

Peppermint - Mental healing, overall purification, psychic awareness, love, and passion.

Pine - Persistence. Increases modesty, prosperity, financial health, and good health.

Quince – Good luck, happiness, protection. Carry quince seeds in a red bag to keep yourself safe from attack.

Raspberry Leaf – Love and romance, temptation, divination.

Red Sandalwood – Used in incense for meditation, healing, and inducing trance work.

Rose – Used in charms of love and beauty, harmony, and divination; it increases self-confidence.

Rosemary – Cleansing, purification and spirituality, vitality and energy, wisdom and knowledge, protection.

Rowan – Protection, enhanced psychic connections.

Rue – Protection, exorcism, purifying, passion charms, and protective charms.

Solomon's Seal Root – All-round protection against evil and negative energy.

Spearmint – Love and passion, psychic strength, cleansing, rebirth, protecting property and belongings.

Star Anise – Divination, good fortune, psychic dreams, travel charms, astral traveling.

Thyme – Inner beauty, strength, courage, a favorite herb of spirits.

Valerian – Protection, removing enemy spells, dispelling negativity, Egyptian magic.

Vervain – Old World herb of wisdom, knowledge, healing, and prophecy.

White Sage – Cleansing, house protection, trance work, healing, and mental clarity.

White Willow Bark – Peace, wisdom, knowledge, attracting love that will last, divination, lunar magic.

Wild Lettuce – Inducing visions, trance, dream magic, astral travel, and improved sleep patterns.

Witch Hazel – Comfort and healing, wisdom, protection, comfort, and dealing with grief, dispels anger and negativity.

Woodruff – Success and achievements. Put woodruff in your left shoe, and your team will win.

Wormwood – Induces psychic vision, connections to the spirit world, strengthens hexes and curses, and removes any negative spells that have been cast against you.

Yarrow - Ancient medicinal flower used for courage, divination, and good fortune.

Conclusion

What a wild ride that was! Hopefully, you are all set for your new magical journey and are looking forward to your future. You have the knowledge, the expertise, and the intent, so all you need now is that first step. Become part of this brave new world filled with positivity and love. Be safe and happy with your crafting, and you will soon be ready to share your new passions with other members of the magical community. There are so many reasons to become involved, so don't wait another minute. Good luck, not that you need it, and enjoy your experiences.

Here's another book by Mari Silva that you might like

Your Free Gift
(only available for a limited time)

Thanks for getting this book! If you want to learn more about various spirituality topics, then join Mari Silva's community and get a free guided meditation MP3 for awakening your third eye. This guided meditation mp3 is designed to open and strengthen ones third eye so you can experience a higher state of consciousness. Simply visit the link below the image to get started.

https://spiritualityspot.com/meditation

References

"11 Popular Tarot Spreads for Beginners and Experts." Www.alittlesparkofjoy.com, 19 July 2021, www.alittlesparkofjoy.com/easy-tarot-spreads/#three-card-tarot-spread.

"13 Best Crystals for Divination." All Crystal, 9 Aug. 2022, www.allcrystal.com/articles/crystals-for-divination/.

"25 Types of Witches: The Magical List of Witchcraft." Facts.net, 4 July 2021, facts.net/types-of-witches/.

Aletheia. "7 Types of Spirit Guides (& How to Connect with Them)." LonerWolf, 5 Feb. 2018, https://lonerwolf.com/spirit-guides/

"Elemental Magic for Beginners: Basic Principles - Craft of Wicca." Craftofwicca.com, 8 Mar. 2019, https://craftofwicca.com/elemental-magic-for-beginners/#Elemental%20Magic%20For%20Beginners

"Gods and Goddesses in Witchcraft: A Beginner's Guide." Witchbox, 22 May 2023, https://witchbox.co.uk/blogs/witchbox-blog/understanding-the-13-gods-and-goddesses-in-witchcraft

Herbs, Colleen Vanderlinden Colleen Vanderlinden. "Evolution and History of Witchcraft Timeline." LoveToKnow, https://paranormal.lovetoknow.com/Witchcraft_History

"How to Cast a Wicca Ritual Magic Circle." The Not so Innocents Abroad, www.thenotsoinnocentsabroad.com/blog/how-to-cast-a-wicca-ritual-magic-circle.

https://www.facebook.com/learn.religions. "What's the Difference between Evoke & Invoke in Paganism?" Learn Religions, www.learnreligions.com/evoke-and-invoke-2561892.

"Learning Tarot: A Complete Tarot for Beginners Guide." Www.alittlesparkofjoy.com, 14 Sept. 2020, www.alittlesparkofjoy.com/tarot-beginners-guide/.

Leavy, Ashley. Crystal Divination: Three Techniques for Insight & Healing - Love & Light School of Crystal Therapy. 19 Aug. 2013, https://loveandlightschool.com/crystal-divination-three-techniques-for-insight-healing/

lynette_starfire. "List of the Most Used Gods in Witchcraft." Witches of the Craft®

"How to Do Ritual Magic - Gain the Power to Create the Life You Choose." Magic Self and Spirit, 14 Feb. 2020, www.magicselfandspirit.com/blogs/magic/how-to-do-ritual-magic/.

May 23, 2020 | Lifestyle. Types of Spirit Guides: The 11 Powerful Guides on Your Team - Typically Topical. https://typicallytopical.com/types-of-spirit-guides

"Moon Magic: A Beginner Crash Course in Lunar Witchcraft." Moody Moons, 4 July 2021, www.moodymoons.com/2021/07/04/moon-magic-a-beginner-crash-course-in-lunar-witchcraft/.

"Prehistoric Witchcraft - Magic Spells." Paranormal Knowledge, 25 Oct. 2020, www.paranormalknowledge.com/magic-spells/prehistoric-witchcraft.html.

"The Ultimate Guide to Magical Herbs for Spells & Rituals - TheMagickalCat.com." Www.themagickalcat.com, 18 Nov. 2020, www.themagickalcat.com/magical-herbs-guide.

"The Wheel of the Year Explained: The Ultimate Guide to Understanding Nature's Sacred Cycles – Small Ripples." Www.smallripples.com, www.smallripples.com/the-wheel-of-the-year-explained/.

Tyler, Deanna. "The Mystery of Nordic Rune Stones." Rune Divination, 18 Sept. 2015, https://runedivination.com/the-mystery-of-nordic-rune-stones/

"Wiccan Deities: A Complete Guide to Wiccan Gods and Goddesses." Explore Wicca, 8 July 2018, https://explorewicca.com/wiccan-deities/

WiseWitch. "Invoking the Gods & Goddesses: Common Sense Counsel." Wise Witches and Witchcraft, 3 Mar. 2018, https://witchcraftandwitches.com/gods-and-goddesses/invoking-gods-goddesses-common-sense-counsel/.

WITCH. "6 Elements (Yes, 6!) - How and Why to Invoke Them in Ritual." WITCH, 1 June 2016, https://badwitch.es/6-elements-yes-6-invoke-ritual

"Your Guide to Rune Divination." Rune Divination, 7 Oct. 2015, https://runedivination.com/your-guide-to-rune-divination